Kingdom Thoughts

Your Roadmap to a Successful Tomorrow

By
Gary Keesee

ISBN 978-1-4675-6705-3

<u>Dedication</u>

_Dedicated to my ministry partners, who are helping to send the Kingdom around the world.
And to my life partner, wife and encourager, Drenda._

Special thanks to the great team of people who helped me compile these Kingdom Thoughts.

Table of Contents

Great!

Introduction

When Drenda and I discovered the Kingdom of God, we were in a bad place: in serious debt, losing money in our business, sick in my body without knowing if I would ever get better. Although Christians for many years, attending church weekly and me having an Old Testament degree, obviously there was something very wrong. It was in our despair that we cried out to God for help and He began to speak to me about learning how His kingdom worked.

Very quickly our lives began to change. I was healed. I launched new businesses and vision sprang up in our hearts. We became debt free and started to give thousands away to Kingdom projects. Our lives were so transformed that there was nothing else that compared to the Kingdom, and we have committed ourselves to helping others learn what we learned. We launched Faith Life Church to mentor people in the Kingdom. We launched our television outreach to extend our reach further and to help more people.

By replacing our thoughts with God's thoughts, we began to expand our vision. By replacing our own human perceptions with Kingdom perceptions, we began to do things we could never do in our own strength. Faith comes by hearing the Word of God, and with faith all things are possible.

As you take the time to read this book, I believe your thoughts about yourself will be replaced with Kingdom thoughts.

This book, *Kingdom Thoughts*, is really produced from the messages that I taught and the blogs that I wrote over a period of a year and a half. We would get many responses and comments each week from the blogs and teachings, so we thought it would be good if we could put it all together in a book that could act as a daily devotional to encourage your faith. The topics vary in this book, but all of them deal with Kingdom principles for life, and I know they will help you walk out your own life with greater impact.

I trust that this devotional book will inspire you to be all you can be.

Will "Finished" Be the Final Word in Your Story?

Easter—to so many, it's simply that day of the year when people dress up and put fancy outfits on their kids and head to church to hear about how Jesus died on the cross for our sins. But His death isn't the most important part of the story. After all, a lot of people die. No, the most powerful message of the Gospel isn't that Jesus died, it's that He rose again. Jesus paid for sin. He overcame death. He gave us liberty. He made us sons and daughters of God Almighty. He gave us amazing benefits. There is nothing greater that has happened in the history of the earth. When he said, "It is finished," as He hung on the cross, He meant that everything God could do for us was done. He gave everything to give us life more abundantly.

I was in Texas for a conference with a pastor who had seen us on television. He told me how he had heard something different when he watched us. He had heard something that got his attention. So , he got some of our CDs. When he came to pick me up, he was driving this big, beautiful, white Ford Excursion truck. I said, "Man! That's a nice truck!" He was so excited. He told me how he had been healed of diabetes and how he had been believing God for a new vehicle. Then a business friend approached him and told him he had rebuilt a truck and that God had told him to give it to this pastor. Now, that's not just a great story. Something had changed for my pastor friend.

Another couple wrote me and told me their story. Jim and Pam had been running a business out of their home for 12 years. They had been blessed over the years, but something was always missing. They were just surviving and they were frustrated. Then they heard some of our teachings on the Kingdom of God and how to live in the Kingdom here on the earth. Five months later, they had gone from barely being able to pay their bills to having 5 employees and quadrupling their monthly income. What had changed for them? What was the difference?

Years ago, before I was pastoring, Drenda and I were living on commissions and nearly bankrupt. We had 10 maxed out credit cards, 3 finance company loans, owed family members $26,000, had judgments and liens against us, owed tens of thousands of dollars to the IRS. Pawnshops were a familiar place to us. The mattresses my boys had in their bedroom were thrown out from a nursing home. Who wants to live like that? We were surviving at the lowest level. We lived that way for 9 years. The stress was pretty apparent. I began to have panic attacks. I lived in a state of fear. It just kept getting worse.

The electric man would come to our house every month to cut off our power, and I'd give him a bad check and try to figure out how to cover it. And, by the way, I had one of those little Christian logos on my checks. We were Christians and we were a mess! I had been raised in the church! I had been to a Christian university! Something was wrong. We were believers, but we didn't have a clue.

One night, in my mind, I heard, "You're finished." I lay across the bed weeping and crying out to God, and He said Philippians 4:19, "My God will meet all your needs according to the riches of his glory in Christ Jesus." God clearly told me, "You don't know how my Kingdom works. You've never taken the time to figure it out."

And, right then, we were committed. We were seeking the Kingdom of God. We started on the journey and God began to teach me the Kingdom and how it operated. We were able to pay off all of our debt in two and-a-half years. We had to pinch ourselves every day. We had gotten accustomed to the emotional fires and always wondering where we were going to find the money. Now, we were learning how the Kingdom operated. I was also healed. We were able to build our house. It was like someone had flipped a switch! Everything was working out. I used to dream about having $10 and not owing anyone. I never thought I would be able to save $100,000, or pay cash for a brand-new car.

The Kingdom is good. I have plenty of stories to share so that you wouldn't just have to take my word for it. I get stories all of the time from people who believe in the power of God to change lives.

When Jesus walked this earth, He showed us what God was all about. Jesus gave His life on the cross to buy us back from evil. As He drew His last breath, He spoke: "IT IS FINISHED!" Then, three days later, He kicked the grave wide open. He defeated death. He defeated EVERY work of darkness. See, plenty of people have heard about Easter, but very few people have experienced it.

So, what have you been believing for? Peace? Restoration? Abundance? Healing? Forgiveness? Name it.

"It is FINISHED!"

Posture Yourself to Prosper

I want to share with you about how you can best posture yourself for increase in the days ahead. Here's the secret: you can't do it in your own strength, but you *can* through the Kingdom of God. As you lean on God to train you in His ways and as you abandon *your* ways of understanding, you will discover a new kind of living. That's just what some fishermen did in the Bible. The story I want to point out to you is found in Luke 5:1-11:

> **One day as Jesus was standing by the Lake of Gennesaret, with the people crowding around him and listening to the word of God, he saw at the water's edge two boats, left there by the fishermen, who were washing their nets. He got into one of the boats, the one belonging to Simon, and asked him to put out a little from shore. Then he sat down and taught the people from the boat.**
>
> **When he had finished speaking, he said to Simon, "Put out into deep water, and let down the nets for a catch." Simon answered, "Master, we've worked hard all night and haven't caught anything. But because you say so, I will let down the nets." When they had done so, they**

caught such a large number of fish that their nets began to break. So they signaled their partners in the other boat to come and help them, and they came and filled both boats so full that they began to sink.

When Simon Peter saw this, he fell at Jesus' knees and said, "Go away from me, Lord; I am a sinful man!" For he and all his companions were astonished at the catch of fish they had taken, and so were James and John, the sons of Zebedee, Simon's partners. Then Jesus said to Simon, "Don't be afraid; from now on you will catch men." So they pulled their boats up on shore, left everything and followed him.

Here we read about Peter, James and John, partners in their own failing fishing business. It was not failing due to their lack of knowledge or experience. No, these guys were professional fisherman and had grown up on the lake fishing. Yet, in spite of their experience, they had labored all night and caught nothing. However, something happened on the lakeshore that day that completely changed their results. They went from catching nothing during an exhausting all-night fishing trip to filling both boats with fish in a matter of minutes. In fact, both boats almost sank! It was a catch so huge that seasoned fisherman stood back in amazement. They probably hadn't even heard stories of a catch like that one before. So as you read this story I am sure you may be thinking, "Hey, I need to know how to tap into that. I need a catch like that myself."

I know what it is like to work as hard as you can work, doing all the right things, but still ending up with empty nets, unable to pay the bills or buy the things your family needs. That was me, until I discovered what Peter, James and John discovered that day. Yes, they discovered Jesus, which is the primary revelation. But they also saw *how Jesus operated* within the laws of the Kingdom and with divine revelation to direct them to that amazing catch. Jesus told them where the fish were at, and suddenly they had an unfair advantage over all the other fishing businesses. Because we are now sons and daughters of God with the Holy Spirit living in us, with the ability to pray in the Spirit and receive mysteries, we too have an unfair advantage. We have the ability to tap into that secret wisdom and knowledge of the Kingdom so that we can find the fish (harvest) we need.

Because the Kingdom of God is real and is a true Kingdom with laws of government and legal operations, we can learn how to tap into those laws that produced those fish that day, kind of like we can tap into the laws of physics to get things done. The Bible says we are heirs of this great Kingdom and within it is everything we would ever need in life (Galatians 4:1-7, 2 Peter 1:3). When we use the word "kingdom," we must remember that it comes from two words, "king" and "dominion." So the word "kingdom" is really implying a government, or the jurisdiction of the king. Or we could say it is where the dominion of the king rules.

 Since God is the Supreme King of all things created, both seen and unseen, His dominion is supreme. Amazingly, through Jesus, He has anointed us to represent His authority (government and dominion) here in the earth realm. By learning how His Kingdom operates and how to exercise His authority here in the earth realm, we can truly walk in the blessing of the Lord in our everyday lives. The Kingdom offers us a new way of living, setting us legally above the laws of the earth-curse system.

The laws of the Kingdom can be compared to the laws that allow aircraft to fly. Although planes are heavier than air and are thus subject to the law of gravity, they are able to float by tapping into another law that *supersedes* the law of gravity—the law of lift.

As we begin to tap into the laws of the Kingdom, we are also able to live above the laws of fear, lack, depression, debt, sickness and so much more. Like a plane flying and tapping into a new, higher law, it can fly above the weather and the storms of life. This is the good news of the Kingdom that is offered to us and the good news we offer to others. Psalm 34:8 says, "Taste and see that the Lord is good."

The problem is that so many of God's children have not tasted of the goodness of God like Peter, James and John did that day on that lake. No wonder they left everything and followed Him. They had nothing that could compare to what they just saw. If the Kingdom could produce that kind of catch, the Kingdom itself was surely a greater catch than any catch they could have hoped for in their own strength.

Drenda and I discovered the Kingdom of God almost 30 years ago. We were like Peter, James and John—running as hard as we could in sales but falling farther and farther behind. We loved God, but after living month-to-month for 9 years and becoming almost bankrupt, we were totally in despair. I was on antidepressants and had no hope of a better tomorrow.

It was then that I had a revelation of the Kingdom and began to discover the laws of that great government. Our lives changed— amazingly. Now out of debt, Drenda and I spend our time sharing with people the good news of God's Kingdom.

Your life can change as well—when you catch the Kingdom!

Power-packed Prayer

Proverb 3:5,6

Trust in the Lord with all your heart and lean not on your own understanding; in all your ways acknowledge him, and he will make your paths straight.

Several years ago, when I was facing some obstacles, I had a dream. I was standing in the desert and in front of me was a straight road surrounded by flat sand. God said, "Walk down the road." So I began walking. Then, all of a sudden, huge cement barriers began to pop up here and there and completely block one side of the road or the other so that I had to dodge them as I walked. Then, someone came up behind me and put a blindfold on me. I said, "How am I going to walk down the road? I can't see where I'm going!" And God said, "By my Spirit."

That's how life is supposed to be lived—by His Spirit.

You see, we're creatures of habit. We think we can do things or can't do things based on who we are and what we've already done. But God wants to help you with *you* because He knows that you can do anything with His help.

Proverb 3:5 tells us to trust in the Lord with our whole heart and lean not on our own understanding. I know that's not always easy to do. But "all" of your ways means ALL of your ways. That means you have to acknowledge that you don't have the answers. That means that you're going to have to trust Him to lead you in life.

You're not going to be able to walk out His plan for your life if you're not listening to what He has to say. That's what prayer is.

Prayer is more than speaking. It's listening.

James 5:13 says, "Is any one of you in trouble? He should pray." Notice it doesn't say "Let him call his best friend, or let him sign up for government assistance or let him Google what to do about his problem." It says PRAY.

If a man's in trouble, he should pray! And don't tell me you can't hear God.

You CAN hear God. People say they don't know how to hear God, but they really do. "What Gary? I don't hear Him ever!" Yes, you do! You just don't know His voice. You haven't taken the time to define His voice and learn the difference, because His voice sounds like your thoughts. You have to learn when it's Him.

You've heard my story. We were dysfunctional financially. I wasn't disciplined to seek out God's Kingdom. God was something I had in my life, but He wasn't my life.

Do you know what I'm talking about? Are you trying to survive like that?

When I hit bottom financially and physically, I had to have answers. And there it is—the difference between how you cry out to God from your heart and how you cry out to God in a religious setting. I HAD to hear God. I HAD to.

And in prayer God began to lead me out of my mess. He'll lead you to victory, too, if you will go before Him with a sincere heart and pray, and ask Him to show you what to do.

Zechariah was a prophet in the time of Nehemiah when they were rebuilding the temple. They were facing an almost impossible task of rebuilding the temple. Everything was stacked against them. When the situation seemed bleak, God spoke to him.

Zechariah 4:6

> **So he said to me, "This is the word of the Lord to Zerubbabel: 'Not by might nor by power, but by my Spirit,' says the Lord Almighty."**

What was God saying? Simply trust me in this, by yourself you cannot do it, but if you will trust me and follow my Spirit, you can do it. We must do the same. We must lean to God and His Spirit to walk out the vision He has given us. But I have found He is faithful and can be totally trusted.

When we leave to go out of town, we always pray for protection over our property. We were getting ready to leave town in our van awhile back, and the Holy Spirit told me to move my car from the gravel driveway and park it in the grass yard. I thought it was odd and did not act on it as we continued to load the van to depart. But the Holy Spirit kept prodding me to move my car to the grass. He didn't let up. So, although I could not understand why, I moved it. When we came home two days later, a windstorm had hit and a big maple tree had fallen across the gravel driveway exactly where my car had sat before I moved it. But my car was untouched, parked safely in the grass yard. I will admit, I was moved by that demonstration of how important it is to hear God on a daily basis.

You have access to that same amazing help, too. The Bible tells us that the Holy Spirit is our Counselor. He's there to help you in life, in business and in your marriage. But you have to acknowledge Him and not lean to your own understanding.

—◆—

> *The Holy Spirit will lead you around trouble. He'll help you win your fights against the enemy. He'll bring provision. But you have to hear God.*

—◆—

We think we can do it ourselves, but we can't. We're not going to do it without prayer. The Holy Spirit will lead you around trouble. He'll help you win your fights against the enemy. He'll bring provision. But you have to hear God.

In Matthew 6, Jesus told us how to pray. We call it the Lord's Prayer. It isn't just meant to be a picture on the wall. He told us not to babble. Your words and the length of your prayer have absolutely nothing to do with you receiving from the Kingdom of God. So, stop begging God. He already knows what you need. He's waiting on you. Won't you make the commitment to hear His voice today?

Pray Like This

Most people view prayer as begging, or hoping, or even as a religious exercise. When people read the Lord's Prayer, they overlook what Jesus is saying. I know I used to, saying it in church every Sunday. Jesus wasn't necessarily teaching us what exact words to pray, He was teaching us HOW to pray. He didn't say, "When you pray, say this…." He said, "When you pray, pray LIKE this…."

Matthew 6:9-13

"…Our Father in heaven…"

We approach God as our Father. What does this mean? If we are His children then we already have access to the whole estate!

Jesus is telling us to approach God as our Father, which means we have access to what He has. We don't have to earn it and we could never deserve it. He has freely given us His glorious riches!

"…Hallowed be your name…"

Praise God!

"Hallowed" is not a word we use in everyday language, but it means great, awesome, holy and revered. The name of Jesus has been given to us, and with it comes the power and authority of heaven! Great is His name! His power is incomprehensible and amazing. What's more amazing is that we bear His name!

"...Your kingdom come, your will be done on earth as it is in heaven..."

As I shared, the word "kingdom" means "King's dominion." Jesus is showing us that it is our job to bring the King's dominion to bear on any situation we may be facing. If you're facing cancer, you need to bring the jurisdiction of heaven into your hospital room and believe that it is God's will for you to be healed according to 1 Peter 2:24. Apply the power of the King's domain in your situation through your words of faith.

"...Give us today our daily bread..."

My kids don't come to breakfast and beg me for food, saying, "Dad, if we clean our room 25 times a day, will you feed us?" No, they are pretty confident. In fact, they simply say, "Pass the cereal, Dad." They aren't shy. They act like they own the place! They even have the nerve to say, "I'll take some more of that, please." Jesus is giving us permission to approach God as our Father and say, "Give me what I need today."

God views prayer as a requisition, based on relationship. An Army sergeant requisitioning for supplies doesn't beg for what he needs because he is not there at his own expense. He confidently submits his request because the Army has stationed him there.

We are ambassadors of the Kingdom of God, and we can boldly request what we need according to James 4:1. Also, Matthew 7:7 says, "Ask and it will be given to you...." It doesn't say to beg and whine, it says to ask.

Matthew 6:25-33 say our Father already knows what we need before we ask, so there's no need to babble like an unbeliever.

People get hung up on the whole prosperity thing and tell me, "How dare you ask God for things! That's so selfish." The Bible wouldn't say to be generous on every occasion if you weren't meant to prosper to a degree beyond paying your own bills. What's selfish is living a life that is consumed with your needs so you can never help someone else. Prosperity isn't about you; it's about giving to God's work and expanding the Kingdom's influence around the world.

> *You don't have to beg for crumbs and hope that God hears if He's not too busy. You have full rights to His estate!*

You don't have to beg for crumbs and hope that God hears if He's not too busy. You have full rights to His estate! Dad pays for it! Because you are His child, God has also made you an heir. You are a co-heir with Christ—which means whatever Jesus has, you have. Whatever Jesus possesses in the estate (the whole thing), YOU HAVE.

Whatever Jesus did, you can do.

If you get this revelation it will simply blow your mind!

There's a way to pray and know we receive. It's the prayer of faith, being confident that God loves us, He's for us and He's given us the authority to bring His Kingdom wherever we are.

"...Forgive us our debts, as we also have forgiven our debtors..."

God's authority can only flow through love. It is who He is and the law of His Kingdom. If we harden our hearts against another person we are basically hardening our hearts against God Himself, which would cut us off from God being able to help us.

God is very clear in this matter. If we want to receive from God we must have God's heart not only towards Him but towards others. If we don't we will not be able to receive from God.

"...And lead us not into temptation, but deliver us from the evil one...."

Remember, Jesus is teaching us how to pray here. We need to receive revelation concerning what the enemy is setting up for our destruction. And, praise God, we do not need to be afraid, for Jesus has completely destroyed the devil's ability to operate against us in this life. But he will always try to gain entrance in our lives through schemes and tricks. The Holy Spirit helps us and warns us. We need to follow the peace of God and pay attention to the little warning check on the inside of us.

Once we were planning a trip to the beach. We were presented with two options, the Outer banks of North Carolina or Nova Scotia, where Drenda's parents own a home. We were leaning toward the Outer banks because the water was going to be warmer there. As we were planning our trip we suddenly felt a check to not go to North Carolina but instead to go to Nova Scotia. This did not make sense to us. The check on the inside would not leave so, although we did not understand it, we drove to Nova Scotia. Once we got there we were surprised that the weather was so warm. As we turned on the TV we were shocked to see a hurricane was at that moment hitting the Outer Banks of North Carolina and the whole coast was under an evacuation order. Amazingly, the hurricane was pushing the warm air up the coast toward Nova Scotia. We enjoyed an unusually warm two weeks there with warm water for swimming.

Again, you need to take the time to pray and listen to the Holy Spirit. He will lead you in life every day about all things big and small.

Robbing God?

Let me tell you something that might go against what you've been taught:

God doesn't need your money.

Malachi 3:8 says, "Will a mere mortal rob God? Yet you rob me. But you ask, 'How do we rob you?' In tithes and offerings."

People interpret that the wrong way. The scripture goes on to say that what God really wants is to *bless* us. So, the people were really robbing God of His ability to bless them. He can't bless us when we cut Him off. It says that we put ourselves under a curse when we're not walking by His covenant and in His ways. He wants us to walk in the blessing and not suffer under the earth-curse system of lack, sickness and disease.

He says, "Test me in this!" Do you hear His heart in that? He's saying, "Let me show you how much I love you! Let me show you how I want to bless you!"

In Luke 15, Jesus teaches about this with the story of the prodigal son. You know the story. The younger son left the father's house by his own free will and found himself bankrupt and hungry. He hired himself out just to survive. That's the key. In his father's house, he had access to all that his father had. Outside of his father's house, he didn't.

Any parallels? So the son woke up one day and realized that even his father's servants were well taken care of with much left over. So he planned to go home and offer to be a hired hand for his father, but when he got there, that's not what happened. His father *ran* to him and hugged and kissed him! If you remember where the son had just come from—the pig pens—you will understand how astonishing this embrace was. In the Jewish culture touching anything that pigs touched made the father unclean. Do you understand? The father made himself unclean on behalf of the son.

Do you see the comparison to God there? This is exactly what God did through Jesus. He came after us when we had nothing to offer, when we were unclean. The father in the story then called for a royal robe to cover his son's shame. He gave him his signet ring, which represented the father's authority, and then he also restored the son's access to the entire estate. He restored his prosperity. The bottom line is that he restored this son as his son, not a servant in his house.

He gave the son a blessing he didn't deserve.

It was the father's pleasure to give him those things despite the son's hireling mentality. And that's how we were all trained— as unworthy hirelings, only fit to be slaves. We think like the son thought, *If I can just work more, work harder then I can become more valuable to God. Then I can justify His love for me because of what I do for Him.* Because of this hireling mentality that we learned in the earth realm, we never relax in Father's house. We do not know how to receive in Father's house. Consequently, we do not know how to live in the blessing of Father's house.

But God wants us to work *with* Him, not for Him. He wants to display us to people for His splendor, for His glory. He wants us to be known as His people because we're blessed.

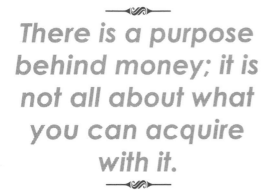

There is a purpose behind money; it is not all about what you can acquire with it.

The father didn't send the prodigal son back out to the streets, wearing torn up clothing and lacking food and shelter. His son bore his name and bore the image of the father himself. If your son walked out in a blizzard with torn clothes and no coat, people would say you're a bad parent. The same is true of God. Where you go, you bear His name. He wants to bless you so that others will see His goodness and come to Him. **What are people saying about Him because of you?**

God wants you blessed and prosperous. There is a purpose behind money; it is not all about what you can acquire with it. God wants you to have His heart. Just as you have received His mercy, He wants you to extend mercy to others and thus be generous on every occasion. When you meet the needs of people, they will see your Father in you and recognize Him, and THANK Him!

Stop robbing God! Start talking about His blessing. Better yet, start demonstrating the blessing of God. Try it!

Seeing From Kingdom Perspective

We need to rewire the way we think.

We have toxic emotions and we use toxic words, and both begin with toxic thoughts. We have to get it straight. We have to stop allowing the enemy to steal our identity, our value and our dreams.

An amazing man of God, and our dear family friend Leif Hetland talked about this recently. He said we have to rewire the way we think. Then he reminded us of David, who was anointed by God, but had to live in a cave. David was in the worst-case scenario, but he changed the environment, and he changed the lives of 400 men. Four hundred men who had lost their identity, dignity, value and dreams—400 so-called losers—were never the same because of David.

1 Samuel 22:1,2

> **David left Gath and escaped to the cave of Adullam. When his brothers and his father's household heard about it, they went down to him there. All those who were in distress or in debt or discontented gathered around him, and he became their leader. About four hundred men were with him.**

What inspired them? They just saw David take out Goliath, the giant. King Saul was quaking in fear; the entire army was quaking in fear—but not David. David took it personally and was offended for God's sake. He was then willing to right the wrong and take Goliath out. Those men wanted change, and they knew that David could also help them face their problems and win. They gathered around David, and the Bible then says that David became their leader. It was not a title; there were no fancy office parks or plush office buildings, no perks or retirement programs. But there was hope, and people will always be drawn to hope.

> *I have found that God will lead you to big problems so He can give you a big answer.*

So here is a truth you need to think about today. When you solve someone's problem, you get a promotion. David solved the problem and he was promoted to become their leader. David did not look at Goliath as a problem but instead as an opportunity. Although David was offended for God's namesake there was more to the story. In 1 Samuel 17:22-29 the Bible records that David asked three times concerning the reward that would be given to the person who took care of the giant. David was motivated by the "giant problem" at hand as an opportunity for his reward. **I have found that God will lead you to big problems so He can give you a big answer.** I always say that God will get the glory and you will get the promotion.

No matter what situation you're in, you can change the environment.

If you have a giant in front of you, consider it an invitation for you to get a promotion. You can either look at that giant and be crippled by fear and insecurity, or you can consider it an opportunity for an upgrade.

Start seeing things from the right perspective. When Jesus got the news about Lazarus, he had a different perspective than everyone else. In John 11:4 we see that Jesus pretty much said, "You're looking at this wrong. This sickness isn't for death, but for the glory of God."

What problem are you fearful over today? See it as an opportunity for you and God to deal with it together. The better you are at handling problems the more problems you can handle. By the way, the world only pays problem solvers. Bigger problem—bigger paycheck.

So Where's Your Peace?

You overslept and you're running behind. You rush around the house yelling at your kids, and snapping at your wife. Then you get into traffic and find yourself slamming your fist on the steering wheel in frustration.

It's been a long day at home with the kids and the laundry is piling up. When they start arguing for what seems like the hundredth time, you scream, "WHY CAN'T I HAVE JUST FIVE MINUTES OF PEACE?"

The world has taught us that having peace in our life is based on the circumstances around us, that we can't have peace in our life as long as we have pressure. But peace isn't the absence of pressure. Peace isn't a *feeling*. Peace is a *person*.

John 14:25-27

> **All this I have spoken while still with you. But the Counselor, the Holy Spirit, whom the Father will send in my name, will teach you all things and will remind you of everything I have said to you. Peace I leave with you; my peace I give you. I do not give to you as the world gives. Do not let your hearts be troubled and do not be afraid.**

What was Jesus' peace? The Holy Spirit. Jesus leaned to the Holy Spirit for everything He did in His ministry. Knowing that He had the ability to get counsel for any and every situation He found Himself in produced a peace that was tangible.

If you spend your life *looking* for peace, you'll find yourself compromising *a lot*. What you need to realize is that you already have peace IN you. No matter what the circumstances are in your life, you have the kind of peace Jesus did—the kind that lets you sleep in the boat while the storm is going on.

Getting that peace requires that you become familiar with the Spirit of God. That takes prayer. You have to know when to step forward and when to step back. When you don't know what to do, you need to pray in the Spirit. The answers won't come by *your* strength or *your* wisdom. They will come by His.

When Israel was released from captivity in Babylon, their task was to rebuild Jerusalem. But they let people intimidate them—they let their circumstances affect their peace—then everything stopped. They didn't build for *16 years*. Although it was an almost impossible task God spoke concerning their plight, we read in Zechariah 4:6 that God said, "Not by might, nor by power, but by my Spirit." That was meant for you, too.

So, where's your peace? Are you rebuking the storms, or thanking God for your umbrella? Wouldn't you rather have a sunny day? Umbrellas are great, but they can't help you all the time. You have to tap into the peace and victory that's only by the Spirit. Then, even when your circumstances seem crazy, when there are storms all around you, or when you're in enemy territory, you'll have peace because you will know exactly what to do. God is there and will lead you with His wisdom.

Think about it. Amen.

Positioned For Promotion?

So you want a promotion. You want to be in charge of something. You believe your purpose in life is to be in leadership. That's great. We all want to have a clear, defined purpose for our lives, but when it comes down to it, are you really ready?

See, the world functions differently than God does. In the world we jockey for positions. We market ourselves. We push to make things happen in our own strength. We expect promotion because of the hours we've put in, the things we've accomplished or the titles we've earned, but that's not how it works in God's system.

Examine the parable of the Shrewd Manager in Luke 16 in the context of life, and it will stop and make you think.

Luke 16:1-8

> **Jesus told his disciples: "There was a rich man whose manager was accused of wasting his possessions. So he called him in and asked him, 'What is this I hear about you? Give an account of your management, because you cannot be manager any longer.' The manager said to himself, 'What shall I do now? My master is taking away**

my job. I'm not strong enough to dig, and I'm ashamed to beg—I know what I'll do so that, when I lose my job here, people will welcome me into their houses.'

So he called in each one of his master's debtors. He asked the first, 'How much do you owe my master?' 'Eight hundred gallons of olive oil,' he replied. The manager told him, 'Take your bill, sit down quickly, and make it four hundred.' Then he asked the second, 'And how much do you owe?' 'A thousand bushels of wheat,' he replied. He told him, 'Take your bill and make it eight hundred.' <u>The master commended the dishonest manager because he had acted shrewdly.</u> For the people of this world are more shrewd in dealing with their own kind than are the people of the light [emphasis mine]."

Notice that the master commended the dishonest manager because he had acted shrewdly. Basically what he was saying is that he had failed in his management on the master's behalf, and he was wasting the master's possessions. Yet when he was faced with a tough situation personally, he was able to be shrewd towards his own profit. The dishonest manager proved that he was able to be shrewd when it profited himself. Being shrewd means creatively thinking of ideas and methods to advance a cause. Yet he had not been shrewd towards the master's purposes.

Read it and you're forced to ask yourself, "What am I trying to do with my energy? Whose kingdom am I trying to build?"

Is the answer your own, or God's?

So many believers want to talk about the anointing and ministry and what's exciting to them, but when it comes to the not-so-exciting stuff, like being faithful and loyal and paying the price, they shut down. You want to know how to get promoted? Read 1 Timothy

3. Paul is telling Timothy how to choose his leadership team. Now, these qualifications are given in light of Timothy choosing spiritual leadership, but this applies to anyone wanting a promotion. It's about management. Read it. Is that you? Do you manage your family properly? How's your home life? Do you take care of your house and your car?

> *God isn't going to speak spiritual direction to you until you qualify by taking care of earthly responsibilities.*

This is so important. Everyone says the right stuff. But go to their car and their house and see how they manage those things. If someone doesn't know how to manage their personal life, how can they manage a corporation, a sales office or a team? **God isn't going to speak spiritual direction to you until you qualify by taking care of earthly responsibilities.** Until you pass these tests, you'll be in a holding pattern. Your resume doesn't matter. No one puts how many pencils they stole or the number of times their boss wasn't happy on their resumes. Forget what you tell people. What are you doing with your life, your relationships and your stuff? You have to handle what you have before you can handle something else.

Now, you can learn management. You can make changes. But authority is another touchy subject that has everything to do with your destiny.

Where do you think God will put you to test you for promotion? Do you think He's looking at how well you pray? NO! He tests you for promotion by placing you under authority and seeing how you do. So, do you mumble under your breath about your boss, or laugh with a friend who got out of a speeding ticket? See, you have to understand how to be *under* authority in order to be *in* authority. God knows that **if you don't obey earthly authorities, you will NOT obey Him.** He's going to keep working on your character and molding you so that you can stay where He's leading you.

So, start submitting to the authorities in your life as unto God. And take stock of your life. Analyze your attitude and your management abilities.

Then, sit down with your family and get things in line. Prune some things if you need to so you can posture yourself to receive promotion. Trust God with who He has placed you under and with what He is leading you to do. Pass the tests and get to your destiny.

So in light of the parable of the dishonest manager, why do you want to prosper? Whose kingdom are you building? Where is your heart?

Stand on the Rock

We believe that the entire Bible from Genesis 1 to Revelation 22 is the story of violent conflict between two unalterably opposed kingdoms. One is ruled over by our Lord Jesus Christ; the other by His adversary and enemy—the devil. Every detail of your life falls within the jurisdiction and operation of one of those two kingdoms. There are no exceptions. Every choice you make increases one kingdom at the expense of the other. So when you choose Christ and you choose the Word of God, it enlarges the reign of Jesus in your heart at the expense of the power of hell in your life. But when you choose the flesh, carnality or sin, you choose the devil and the reign of the devil in your life. One area that you have been given victory through what Jesus did is in the area of healing.

I want to share a story of a friend of mine regarding experience with the Word of God in this area. But it's not just any story—it's an example of two people who had confidence in the Word of God and can tell you how to get there, too.

In April 2002, Ted was having some symptoms. He was bleeding. When his doctor performed a colonoscopy, Ted heard him say, "Oh my God, look at that tumor. Have you ever seen one that big?" Ted had a cancerous tumor.

But in that moment, Ted took comfort in the Word of God and the promises of God. Then he and Ginny went home and prayed. And prayed. And prayed some more.

Then they began doing the things you do when you get a report like that. They got information. They went to specialists. Finally, the doctors told Ted that he would need to have surgery—but not just any surgery. This resectioning would cut off the function of everything south of Ted's belly button—his bowel, bladder and erectile function would be cut off. Ted says that, in that moment, he looked at Ginny and she looked at him, and then they both looked at the doctor and told him not to schedule that surgery. They both knew they needed time with God—they needed to seek His face. And they did.

Ted went to his church and lay right in the front on his face praying in the Spirit and asking God what in the world he was going to do.

And for the first time in 40 years of ministry, God plainly gave Ted a word—Proverb 3:16—"Long life is in [wisdom's] right hand. In [wisdom's] left hand are riches and honor." Then God spoke to Ted and said He would give him wisdom to deal with this situation. God told Ted that if he did the wisdom he would be healed within one year, but if he chose not to do the wisdom God said, "I'll see you soon."

Now, I know you're thinking: *What in the world? This guy was told he has a giant tumor in his gut and now he thinks God is talking to him?* That's exactly what happened and that's exactly what God does—if you ask Him.

See God doesn't say, "You idiot, why are you talking to me about this?" He's happy for you to ask Him. That's what Ted did.

He asked God. And God answered.

> *Storms are going to come. Life is happening. What are you going to do when life is happening to you and it comes to your house? Are you going to stand on the Rock?*

God told Ted what he should eat and what he should drink. Ted became a vegan and he changed his workaholic lifestyle. He got healthier and healthier and healthier. God told Ted his way of escape from colon cancer. It was very strict and Ted didn't like it. But God didn't bother to ask Ted's opinion—as Ted says, "He thinks He's God. He thinks our role is to obey. If we want to receive His promise, we have to do what He says. God has a way of escape but it's not always the way we want."

By December, the tumor had shrunk by 50-70 percent. Ted continued the program he was on and, in April, he went back to the specialist. This time, he showed Ted the screen and said, "That's where the tumor was. It's not there. As a matter of fact, I can't even see any evidence that it was ever there."

Ted trusted God. He sought the wisdom of God. He obeyed. And one year later—just like God said—Ted didn't have cancer anymore.

So what's the difference between Ted and anyone else? Why did Ted receive his healing when other people don't? What do you need to do to get this kind of healing?

1.   Figure out how you find God—how you touch God. Learn this while you're not in crisis. For some people it's reading the Bible over and over again; for some it's worship; for some it's tongues. Figure it out and do it. One of the very first things Ted and Ginny did was go into prayer. They knew how to reach God. You can't tap into the wisdom, resources and authority of God if you can't reach Him.

2.   Don't be weak in the Kingdom of God. Build a foundation on the Word of God—the Rock. Be prepared. When you have sickness and disease come into your life you better know what Jesus is about and what the devil is about. Don't be confused about it. As Ted said, "Oral Roberts used to tell us God is a good God and the devil is a bad devil, and don't get it mixed up."

3.   Don't entertain unbelief. When that thing knocks on your door send it away. If you let it in there and entertain it, it will get harder and harder. When unbelief does pop into your mind, repent of it. Don't say it's too hard or it's not fair. That's unbelief and unbelief is sin. The only way to get sin out of your life is to repent. Sin doesn't just disappear because you're being good. You have to repent and take responsibility. You have to change. Turn around and go another way.

4.   Do whatever it takes to keep building your faith. Drive around and declare healing scriptures at the top of your lungs like Ginny did, or look up every scripture on healing—write them on your bathroom mirror. Do whatever it takes.

5.   Listen to what is coming out of your mouth. It will tell you where your faith is. It will tell you what's in your

heart. Listen and fix it. Learn how to speak the Word of God—it's the only offensive weapon we've been given. Confess the Word. Declare the Word. Declare the expected end. God calls things that be not as though they are, and that's what you need to do. Say it.

6.   Listen to what God is saying and OBEY. God's got a word for you. He's got a revelation for you in whatever circumstance you find yourself. You must have confidence that He will make a way for you—He'll make a way of escape for you.

Pastor Ted and Ginny did all of these things. They learned to trust God in the hard place.

Storms are going to come. Life is happening. What are you going to do when life is happening to you and it comes to your house? Are you going to stand on the Rock? Are you going to have faith and trust God and find a way of escape, or is your house going to fall down?

Stepping Out

1 Corinthians 2:9

> However, as it is written: No eye has seen, no ear has heard, no mind has conceived what God has prepared for those who love him—but God has revealed it to us by his Spirit.

As we give and trust God for increase, we don't usually know where that increase will come from, but God will reveal it to us. The key is that it usually is from someplace we haven't thought of, heard of or seen as a part of our lives. This is the exciting part of walking in faith with God.

When Drenda and I agreed to give $200,000 to our church's building campaign, I think we had about $15,000 to sow towards that goal at the start of the campaign. I really didn't see any way that I would be able to make my goal in the natural. About two months after we released our faith, the Lord brought an idea to me in prayer. I own businesses. One of my businesses was involved with a vendor that had a bonus program for which my company did not qualify. Two years earlier, I had asked the Vice President about it, and she made it clear that the structure of our business and our relationship with our vendor did not qualify for that bonus pay. I asked again a year later and she was still very firm that there was no way to qualify for this bonus.

But now, in prayer, I heard the Lord say to go back to them and request the bonus pay one more time. I was hesitant to do so since the last time I had done that, the Vice President made her position very clear, but I went ahead and e-mailed my request to her and made my case why I thought my company should qualify. Two weeks later, I received her response—she had changed her mind and I would be getting the bonus! Amazingly, this bonus would pay me $200,000 in additional revenue over the next three years! Now remember, I had no idea where the money was going to come from, but God made a way with a direction that was extraordinary and unknown to me at the time.

You have to know that God will do the same for you. If you'll step out—if you'll submit your finances to God—you'll find out that God will meet you there with ideas and direction that you've never thought of, seen or heard before. Imagine the entire Body of Christ all moving this way at the same time. Wow! Remember, stretch your faith, do what you are led to do, and let God do what He does!

Close the Door to the Enemy

1 Peter 5:8

> **Be self-controlled and alert. Your enemy the devil prowls around like a roaring lion looking for someone to devour.**

Many of us are familiar with this scripture in 1 Peter where we learn that our enemy the devil prowls around like a roaring lion looking for someone to devour. What is he really looking for? He's constantly seeking an entry point, a loophole, an opportunity made available by our sin or neglect to bring storms into our lives.

Storms blow through our lives for many reasons. They can occur as a result of our neglect, willful disobedience or carnal thinking. In fact, the opening Satan uses to gain entrance into our lives may be the result of something that seems small, insignificant and trivial to us. But if you find yourself in the midst of a storm—when your expectations don't match your results—that's when you need to go to God and ask Him to reveal the area causing the storm.

As God shows you where the breach has occurred, confess your sin or your neglect, and close the door so the devil no longer has a legal right to bring storms into your life. Rebuke the enemy and remain firmly convinced that he will flee from you.

Be self-controlled and stay alert to avoid giving Satan anymore footholds in your life! Listen and OBEY when the Holy Spirit prompts you to take action, be still, avoid a situation or correct something in your life.

Then, stand boldly on the promise that since God is for you, no one—or nothing—can stand against you. And remember that you're covered by the blood of Jesus! Rest in the confidence that, as you ask in faith, God hears you and you will have what you ask for.

Remember, you are standing in the finished work of Christ. Your feelings have nothing to do with it. This is a legal matter!

Authority

We've all been there, in the break room when someone was mumbling under their breath about the boss, or out for coffee with a friend who was laughing off an unpaid parking ticket or at the playground when a kid talked back to his parent—but what did you think when it happened? Did you shrug it off as normal? Or did you recognize that it wasn't right?

We talked about how our enemy—Satan—roams around looking for an opportunity to interfere with our lives. We learned the most powerful key to preventing storms in our lives—respecting and honoring authority.

Most believers can discern that they've sinned against God, but they fail to recognize when they've sinned against people, the relationships or the authorities in their lives. And there it is—the opportunity Satan was looking for to bring the storms into their life.

The culture tells us that we get to judge whether or not a person is worthy of honor and respect, but the Bible says there is no authority except that which God has established. What does that mean? It means we don't get to choose. We are to honor and respect those in authority whether we like them or not and whether we agree with them or not.

No example shows us this better than that of David and Saul. Remember that Saul wanted David dead. Yet we read that when David had an opportunity to kill Saul, he was conscience-stricken. Yes, he knew that Saul was trying to kill him, but he also knew that Saul was God's anointed. He still respected the position and the authority of the king. David knew it was not his place to deal with Saul—it was God's place.

> *Pray for those that have authority over you—leadership is a lot harder than you think it is. And realize that as you humble yourself to an authority, you are saying yes to God.*

Not one of us is outside of authority. How you relate to the authorities God has placed over you speaks volumes about your character and your future.

Don't help Satan discredit your employer, your pastor, your spouse, a government official or any other authority in your life. Instead, humble yourself and give them the honor and respect that is due them not because of who they are but because Jesus is your Lord.

Pray for those that have authority over you—leadership is a lot harder than you think it is. And realize that as you humble yourself to an authority, you are saying yes to God.

Take the 30-day Challenge

Did you know that the Kingdom of God interfaces in the earth realm through our hearts and is released through our mouths? When I first began teaching this I saw many people healed through the same principles of believing, speaking and receiving healing.

I've continued to see evidence of people applying those principles. I want to share one of those stories with you. I want you to read her story carefully. Then, I want you to grab hold of it and realize that the same promises that brought her story to pass are available to you also. Because God is no respecter of persons—you have the exact same legal rights as Cortney does.

When Cortney was about 12 years old, her right leg had grown longer than her left leg. Her left leg was about 2 inches shorter than her right leg, and her left foot was smaller then her right foot. As you can imagine, this caused Cortney a lot of problems. She couldn't run. She said trying to buy a pair of shoes was a joke. The difference was so drastic that she would have to stand off balance. In fact, she could stand on her right leg and swing her left leg. It was that bad.

The unevenness of Cortney's legs caused her a lot of pain,

especially after she was married and got pregnant. She dealt with horrible pain during both her first and second pregnancies. But then Cortney heard my daughter Amy's story. Amy had a 13-pound tumor disappear out of her body when she told it to leave.

When Cortney heard Amy's story and how Amy had originally settled for a doctor's report, she realized she had done the same. She also realized that she shouldn't be limping and off balance. Cortney knew that wasn't what God had promised her. So, she started speaking to her body and telling it to line up. But something was wrong. It didn't work. So, she asked God why and He showed her. He showed her that she had some anger and resentment that she had been holding onto. She needed to forgive and let go. God showed her that she couldn't be healed in her body until she was healed emotionally. So Cortney took the journey of forgiveness.

And one morning she was in the shower and she realized she was standing straight. She even tried to stand crooked to see if she was imagining things. She yelled for her husband to come and confirm it. Cortney had received her healing!

Now, Cortney was raised in church. She believed in healing. She knew it was true. She knew the power of God. She had even spoken it over other people. So, what was the problem? Cortney had to receive the healing that was already available. It was up to her to accept what was being offered to her. She had to tell herself that God had already healed her. She had to change her picture.

What are you painting your mental picture with? Are you painting it with what the media says, with the doctor's reports or with the Word of God?

How about your eye gate? What are you allowing into your heart through your eyes? What are you looking at on the computer? What are you watching on television? Are all those carnage and murder stories really worth it? Dr. Diana Morgan, who teaches at our Bible college, says television is called such because it's "telling a vision." What vision are you getting programmed with?

Then there's your mouth. What are you speaking over yourself? What are you saying about your children or your spouse? Do you know that you're giving those words control over your heart?

We have to be transformed by the renewing of our minds.

So how do we do that? We start with the Word of God. We find scriptures to reprogram our mind and repaint our picture. We speak the Word of God.

Do this. Make a decision to reprogram your mind. Take the next 30 days to reprogram your mindset about a particular area of struggle. This is what my daughter Amy calls the 30-day Challenge, and this is what she did to overcome that tumor. She had to repaint a picture of herself healthy, and she had to reject that doctor's report as the final say. God's Word is the final say in your life! Reprogram your mindset for that picture of health, *or whatever it is that you're believing God for.*

Write down the scriptures you're standing on.

Then, every single morning, noon and night, or whenever you have fear, pain or sickness or you get a bad report, pull those scriptures out. Study them. Read them out loud. Reprogram your picture.

For some of you, it may only take 10 days. For some of you, it may take the full 30 days. For some of you, it may take a year to get all the junk out of your heart and really reprogram your picture. No matter how long it might take, Drenda and I challenge you to take the challenge.

Take the 30-day Challenge and dare to believe that God is true to His Word. He is faithful.

Amen.

The Big Misconception

What happens when you die?

Now brace yourself, because there's a huge misconception among believers.

You WILL be judged.

Hebrews 9:27 tells us that people are destined to die and then face judgment. Matthew 12:36 tells us that everyone will have to give account on the Day of Judgment.

Yes, *everyone.*

But let me help set the record straight. If you are a believer you won't be judged on whether or not you're going to hell; you'll be judged according to your *works.*

Surprised? Look it up:

- Revelation 20:13 says we'll be judged according to what we've done.

- In 1 Peter, we read that we need to conduct ourselves in fear and reverence.

- Matthew 16:27 says, "For the Son of Man is going to come in his Father's glory with his angels, and then he will reward each person according to what he has done."

- Revelation 22:12 says each person will be given to according to his works.

According to every person's works, God is going to reward and judge. Of course, you're not saved by works. Ephesians 2:8-9 confirms that. But your belief determines *where* you spend eternity. Your behavior, your deeds, your acts will determine *how* you spend eternity. In heaven, you'll be rewarded for your deeds. In hell, you'll be punished for your deeds.

In Luke 16:19-25, Jesus gave an insight into what happens to people when they die:

> **There was a rich man who was dressed in purple and fine linen and lived in luxury every day. At his gate was laid a beggar named Lazarus, covered with sores and longing to eat what fell from the rich man's table. Even the dogs came and licked his sores.**
>
> **The time came when the beggar died and the angels carried him to Abraham's side. The rich man also died and was buried. In Hades, where he was in torment, he looked up and saw Abraham far away, with Lazarus by his side. So he called to him, "Father Abraham, have pity on me and send Lazarus to dip the tip of his finger in water and cool my tongue, because I am in agony in this fire."**
>
> **But Abraham replied, "Son, remember that in your lifetime you received your good things, while Lazarus received bad things, but now he is comforted here and**

you are in agony. And besides all this, between us and you a great chasm has been set in place, so that those who want to go from here to you cannot, nor can anyone cross over from there to us."

Now, in verse 22, "the time came when the beggar died and the angels came and carried Lazarus to Abraham's side." Notice there wasn't a judgment. Neither the rich man nor the beggar went before a judge to decide where they went.

They weren't taken before a throne and a judgment given. So, who made the decision on where they went? They did. And you will decide *where* you go. Then you will face judgment. Your works will be judged.

So, it DOES matter how you live on the earth.

First Corinthians 5:10 says,

> **For we must all appear before the judgment seat of Christ; that every one may receive the things done in his body, according to that he hath done, whether it be good or bad.**

Notice, it says nothing about heaven. Paul is talking about receiving what he is due for what he has done in his life. This judgment is to discern rewards.

First Corinthians 3:10-15 sheds a lot of light:

> **By the grace God has given me, I laid a foundation as a wise builder, and someone else is building on it. But each one should build with care. For no one can lay any foundation other than the one already laid, which is Jesus Christ. If anyone builds on this foundation using gold, silver, costly stones, wood, hay or straw, their work will be shown for what it is, because the Day will bring it to**

light. It will be revealed with fire, and the fire will test the quality of each person's work. If what has been built survives, the builder will receive a reward. If it is burned up, the builder will suffer loss but yet will be saved— even though only as one escaping through the flames.

See, we have the foundation that holds the house up—Jesus Christ. Our belief as Christians gives us that foundation that will always be there. But when you receive Christ, you not only get the foundation, but you begin to build on it. Paul is telling us to be careful how we build because the "Day" will bring it to light and test the quality of our building—of our work. What we choose to build upon that foundation will be tested.

You have the choice to build on that foundation with gold (an eternal metal) by caring about eternal things and making decisions based on things of eternal value, or you can build with wood, hay and straw by making decisions based on things that are temporary.

See, God designed you. He created you for a specific place, time and purpose. And you will have to answer for your uniqueness. Did you answer the call on your life? Did you finish your race? Or are you just going along with life? If so, you're going to miss out on some great rewards!

Now, I'm not talking about becoming some wacked-out Christian. We have this idea in churches that everything spiritual is fluffy and goofy and makes no sense. But that's not God. He's pretty practical. He says, "Love your wife." He says, "Respect your husband." He says, "Take care of your family." He's holding you responsible. You're going to give an account to Him for your life.

And He's going to reward you. Heaven has varying degrees of

position and reward, and hell has varying degrees of punishment. Someone like Hitler isn't going to have the same punishment as someone who was a nice person but staunchly stood against Christ.

The Bible is also very clear in Matthew 6 that you can do good things in the earth and still lose your reward so we know it's a heart issue as well, not just an action issue.

First John 2:28 tells us to continue in Him, so that when He appears we may be confident and unashamed before Him. I believe many Christians will be ashamed before Him, though, for wasting their lives, for making bad decisions and for not being about the Kingdom.

Many years ago, my wife and I were in a contest to win a trip to Hawaii. We missed winning the trip by two sales. We called our national sales director and practically begged him to get us a slot, but it was filled. I really wished I could have gone back and been more diligent, made just two more sales.

I believe that's how it's going to be on the "Day." When you stand in His presence and His glory and everything is laid out before you, do you want to say, "I wish I would have…"?

The Birth of Change

2 Corinthians 5:17

Therefore, if anyone is in Christ, he is a new creature; the old has gone, the new has come!

For freedom to take over our lives we must first recognize where we are living in bondage or if we are living below the freedom that God desires. The best place to find God's will here is His Word, and when we find our lives do not match up to what God says, we must then look intently at ourselves and ask God to show us how to change.

I have been in the ministry now for more than 20 years, and I have learned that people do not change unless they are either forced to or they have a strong desire to. For instance, I know of a man that smoked for over 20 years. Although he wanted to quit he just couldn't seem to muster the strength to do so. During a routine physical, his doctor told him that if he kept on smoking he would die an early death. That man has not had a cigarette since that day. The doctor was the catalyst of change that he needed. However, we do not have to come to a dangerous or pressured place to make changes in our lives—sometimes that may be too late.

Romans 12:2 gives us a mandate to change: "Do not conform any longer to the pattern of this world, but be transformed by the renewing of your mind." Paul is talking about renewing our minds to the thoughts of God. The word "transformed" here is from the Greek word from which we get our word metamorphosis. When we think of metamorphosis, we think of a caterpillar becoming a butterfly. A caterpillar is very limited in its ability to go far; but a Monarch butterfly flies thousands of miles, all the way to Mexico during winter and back again, without ever having been there before. A butterfly soars over the limitations of the earth-bound caterpillar. In the same way, God has given us His Kingdom, which is in us. By applying these new Kingdom laws, we can walk in life with success and above the limitations of our past. We are truly new creatures in Christ Jesus!

Make a list of what you want to change about your life. Then take each item and find a scripture or two pertaining to it, and place those scriptures where you can memorize them. Allow the Spirit of God to show you how to change.

Amen.

Make a list of All the things you want to change. Not just one!

32 Degrees Fahrenheit

Compromise. Absolutes. Can we really live in 50 shades of gray, or are there black and white principles to which we must pay attention?

See, I don't believe that people decide to destroy their lives on purpose. I believe they make a few compromises here and there and that's where they end up. Because as little kids we all played at victory. We didn't play divorce court or bankruptcy court. We played the superhero, the president or whoever we looked up to. We played at winning.

You know why? Because God made us for success. We were created to win. But the enemy doesn't want that. He doesn't want you to win. He wants you to get wrapped up in the world— full of compromises and lies. But God has given us the truth, and the truth is like ice.

See, the conditions have to be just right for ice to form. It only happens at a specific temperature—32°F. It's a fact. God's righteousness is like that. He is very exact. Everything operates with precision. It's an exact formula. There is no gray area. There is no variable. He's designed life to be lived according to the Laws of His Kingdom—according to His Word—a specific temperature.

So the Word of God is our 32°F. His Word is the thermometer that monitors the temperature in our freezer to make sure it stays at 32°F; it's how we measure the temperature of our heart.

So what happens? How does our temperature get off? Well, we've learned before that the enemy prowls around like a roaring lion. He's looking for you. His goal is to get you to move off of 32°F because that's where your covenant is, and he can't do anything to you until he gets you outside of the covenant.

Our foolishness helps him along. You make just one wrong choice. You take just one peek at that website. You tell just one lie. You have just one thought about your attractive co-worker. You decide just this once to go to that certain place with those certain friends. You let things go too far and, before you realize it, you're no longer at 32°F.

And 34°F or 35°F isn't cold enough. That's not how it works. It only takes a degree, or 2 or 3 to completely miss it.

But the world tells us otherwise. They tell us there is no absolute—that 34°F or 35°F is okay and we buy it. We watch the trash on TV and in the theaters, we see it online and we live it. We get accustomed and we stop noticing that we're at 34°F or 35°F. We can't tell the difference. We feel the same and we think everything is great. We let the world tell us that sliding from the 32°F mark is okay, and we're leading the next generation to believe it, too. We're asleep at the wheel.

The dictionary defines sleep as a natural and periodic state of rest during which consciousness of the world is suspended. Spiritual sleep is no different. Our consciousness of God is suspended. We have to recognize it before it's too late.

Now, we're all weak. We've all made mistakes. Before I was a pastor I lied; I copied a friend's paper in college. I've done my share of immature things. But I've let the Holy Spirit correct me. I've let Him deal with me.

> *So the Word of God is our 32°F. His Word is the thermometer that monitors the temperature in our freezer to make sure it stays at 32°F; it's how we measure the temperature of our heart.*

You have to let Him deal with you. Wake up to what's going on around you! Be self-controlled and alert. Confess. Come clean. Say, "I love God. I don't want to do that."

Humble yourself before God. Trust Him. Take the time to learn His Word—to find out what He says. Renew your mind.

Step up and be the church of Jesus Christ. Step up and be free. Get back to 32°F and stay there. Then see where He takes you.

A Life of Giving

2 Corinthians 8:1-7

> And now, brothers we want you to know about the grace that God has given to the Macedonian churches. Out of the most severe trial, their overflowing joy and their extreme poverty welled up in rich generosity. For I testify that they gave as much as they were able, and even beyond their ability. Entirely on their own, they urgently pleaded with us for the privilege of sharing in this service to the saints. And they did not do as we expected, but they gave themselves first to the Lord and then to us in keeping with God's will...just as you excel in everything—in faith, in speech, in knowledge, in complete earnestness and in your love for us—see that you also excel in this grace of giving.

I've met many Christians who say, "When I have money, then I'll tithe and give offerings" or "Well, if I had my car and credit cards paid off, then I would help others" or "I hear my church needs money for their building fund, but how can I give to that when I have a house payment due?" The fact is if you're not faithful with the small amount you do have, you can never be trusted with more. (See the Parable of the Talents in Matthew 25.)

When my family and I were struggling financially we had to make a decision to tithe and give offerings even when it hurt. The fact is we HAD to give if we ever wanted to tap into something greater than what we could do on our own. And believe me, we could not dig ourselves out of our financial mess on our own. We had to trust God that He knew what He was doing when He said to "Give and it shall be given unto you…" (Luke 6:38).

One of the most important decisions you or your family will make will be the decision about your personal giving commitments. Obviously, everyone doesn't have the ability to give the same amount in dollars, but God does call us to make the same quality of commitment, because after all, our lives don't belong to us anyway. Most of us can give far more than we think, whether to our church, a ministry or to our neighbor who is struggling. Each of us has a choice to make:

- We can give based on <u>reason</u>. This means we look at what we have, figure out what is "reasonable" and give that amount. It takes little faith to give by reason. Reason simply asks, "What can I afford?"

- We can give based on <u>revelation</u>. This means we determine our gift by praying, "Lord, what do you want to give through me?" This requires faith. When you make giving a matter of prayer, your decision becomes an act of worship. Revelation giving is asking, "How much am I willing to trust God?" Paul said of the Macedonians in 2 Corinthians 8:3, "They gave not only what they could afford, they gave more than they could afford!"

Prayerfully consider the following suggestions for determining God's will for your giving:

1. Begin by praying every day, "Lord, I want to give myself entirely to you. Now, please show me how to give a gift that will stretch my faith." If you are married, pray together with your spouse.

2. Give yourself time when it comes to making a big decision or giving a huge, faith-stretching amount! Don't rush your decisions. You'll find that the longer you genuinely pray, "Show me how," the more ways God will show you, and you'll be able to give more than the first amount that popped into your head. Allow God to show you how to grow in the grace of giving.

3. Consider creative ways you can give as well, such as:

Increased Giving with Increased Income
Believe God to increase your income as you sow into His Kingdom. Follow the leading of the Holy Spirit as you're sensitive to open doors. Expect the unexpected and watch for opportunities to open up before you. If you're a businessman, believe God to send new clients your way and open up bolder ventures.

Find the Financial Fragments
Look for areas in your life that may be areas of loss financially. Are you paying out unnecessary dollars in any particular area? Is there a source of revenue you've been overlooking? Maybe it's something as simple as turning off the lights when you leave the room.

Personal Property

Did you know you can donate tangible property such as jewelry, coin collections, art, cars, property or almost anything of value to a ministry or church? You can also cash in points through airlines, credit cards, etc. for cash or Visa gift cards in many cases.

Appreciated Stock

When you donate stock you own, either public or private, you can avoid the capital gains tax.

Appreciated Property

You can donate vacant land which you've inherited or purchased, or a vacation house to a non-profit organization.

Contribution from Your IRA

If you are over 59½ years old, you may be able to gift a portion of your IRA to your church and not pay income tax on the portion you withdraw.

However God leads you to give, remember that giving is an essential part of the Christian life because it opens up the windows of heaven and gives God legal access into your finances, which represent your life. If you are embarking on a new journey, such as starting a new business or making a new commitment to your family vision, giving is a great way to begin. Givers are happier people because when we give we operate in the nature of God. John 3:16 says, "For God so loved the world that He GAVE His only son...."

Gather as a family, or with other believers, and pray about what God would have you to do. Resist fear and trust that God's grace will help you bring it to pass.

Access Your Heavenly Purse

Luke 12:32

Fear not, little flock, it is your Father's good pleasure to give you the Kingdom. (KJV)

People tend to get nervous when you start talking about money or giving. They see giving as losing something. Interestingly enough, right after Jesus tells the disciples not to fear, He tells them to sell their possessions and give to the poor. He called it making purses for themselves that would not wear out, a treasure in heaven that will not be exhausted, where no thief or moth can destroy. Then He really gets to the heart of the matter when He says, "Where your treasure is, there will your heart be also."

Now, I don't know about you but I carry a wallet, or at least a money clip. Without a wallet or purse, it's difficult to make financial transactions almost anywhere. When Jesus spoke to us to make a purse for ourselves in heaven, He was helping us to see that as we give in His name, putting our treasure toward heaven's causes, we have an access point through which to make Kingdom transactions.

Remember, Satan claims all the money in the earth as his in

Luke 4. But as we give to God, He will give us insight and concepts on how to capture money. The coin that Peter caught in a fish's mouth was money that was not owned by anyone, so God could legally have Peter catch it. God can't take money from someone else and give it to you; you must legally create money through an idea, or capture it in the marketplace. As we give to God, the windows of heaven are legally opened for us.

Become a giver today. Start using the system of God's purse that never wears out!

Once you start using God's system of finances, I promise you'll be hooked! It works *every time* because, as a child of God, you actually own the whole Kingdom. When you start to think about the resources that are backing you, you'll begin to dream bigger dreams.

At one time in my life a hundred dollars was a lot of money, not that it isn't significant now, but now I must believe God for millions to do what we currently are doing in ministry. As I get comfortable trusting God for that money, my vision will also increase, which will demand even more money. So, we really need to practice tapping into that Kingdom Jesus was talking about. We need to learn to use the purse He talked about, or we may find ourselves like someone who has forgotten to take his or her wallet to the store. We all know how well that works! So remember, Jesus says you already have it. You just have to remember to use your purse.

Become a giver today. Start using the system of God's purse that never wears out!

Are We In God's Economy or the Earth's Economy?

I am sure you have heard Christians comment about the economy, stating the latest problem and then saying, "Boy, I sure am glad that I am not part of the world's economy. I'm in God's economy." That statement is not 100 percent true, yet it does have truth to it. Yes, we have been born again and the principles and laws of the Kingdom of God are now ours to use. However, we live on the earth, within a government. I'm in the United States. Money itself is a product of the United States government, and all commerce (the creation of money) will take place within and be governed by the laws set forth by the United States government.

For years the church has made people believe that they should not be involved with the government or that the government was somehow their enemy or was evil. That is not true at all. Righteous government provides peace and protection, which then allows us to prosper. If you do not believe me, check out nations whose governments are corrupt or immoral. You will find a poverty-stricken nations with bribery and corruption in high places.

Last year I traveled to Naples, Italy. As we were driving around, our tour guide would not let us out of the bus on many occasions because it was not safe. It is a fact that about 20 percent of the

Italian GNP is derived from the black market. In Naples, even a street beggar has to pay a bribe to beg. In the same year I traveled to Albania where parents bribe teachers to pass their children in school. Everyone carries cash for a bribe in case they are stopped by the police. Nations that have no stability provide no way for their citizens to build lasting wealth. Although America has some huge financial and moral issues, as believers, we do not need to jump on the bash America bandwagon, but instead, we need to be proclaiming God's principles, which provide security, peace and stability in every arena of our culture.

It is a fact that we will prosper in any economy by tapping into the laws of the Kingdom; however, where we prosper, and many times the degree to which we can enjoy our success, will depend on the earthly government to which we submit ourselves.

We must pray for and be involved in bringing righteousness to our government. We cannot have the attitude that it doesn't matter what happens "out there" as long as we are safe "in here." If we do not bring light to the darkness, eventually the darkness will become so strong it will be difficult to overcome. A government and an economy can become so corrupt that it becomes difficult for prosperity to come. We are in the world, not of it. But until we are in heaven, we are here on a mission, and yes, we are still participating in the world's economy. We are simply bringing God's economy to bear upon this economy, giving us an advantage over the enemy's ways of obtaining wealth. We mustn't forget to let our light shine in these often ignored segments of society. God needs a righteous voice!

Accelerate Into Your Destiny

Do you ever feel like the way you're doing things now just can't keep up with the vision you see for your life? You may have dreams you want to accomplish, but even though you're working as hard as you can, those dreams seem no closer. There are many roadblocks out there right now: job loss, financial chaos, changing times, busyness and thousands of others excuses. There's only one thing that can break through those walls standing in your way and accelerate you into that new territory: the power of God.

Recently, God spoke to me about acceleration and breakthrough. God also showed me Hebrews 11:33: "...who through faith conquered kingdoms, administered justice, and gained what was promised...."

The path to our dreams can be accelerated through faith, conquering (confronting the issues), administration and justice. I want to tell you two amazing stories of the impossible becoming possible through these principles.

Jennifer's baby was born dead. The midwife could do nothing. Neither could the paramedics. But in the midst of those first few moments of panic, Jennifer turned to her husband and said calmly,

"Don't you say a word. This baby will be fine." See, she had been studying faith, and she knew God was bigger than death. She also knew life and death were in the power of words. (Proverb 18:21.) Jennifer's faith was strong, even when a nurse told her, "Your baby is in a body bag." Amazingly, half an hour after the birth, with no form of life and without resuscitation, the baby awoke!

Tim was an architect who, like many in this economy, lost his job. He refused to stop tithing, so for the months he was out of work, Tim tithed his time doing construction at his church. After long weeks of job-hunting with no success, God led him to pursue his dream of starting his own company designing custom homes. It was the worst possible time to think of starting his own company, but he was sure he had heard God. Sure enough, projects started coming in, even in the midst of the recession.

After hearing this teaching on acceleration, Tim decided to believe for one of his home designs to get built in the most exclusive home showcase in Ohio, the Parade of Homes. He stood on Mark 11:24, knowing that *every* architect in Ohio wanted this opportunity. When Tim called a builder friend and was offered a design in the show, he was elated. But that's not all. Soon after, Tim was asked to design *another* home in the 2010 showcase! Tim continued to believe God for even bigger things. Then in January, Tim was asked by a different builder to design yet *another home* in the Parade. Within a half a year, Tim went from being jobless to owning his own business, with THREE homes showcased in the pinnacle of architectural displays. An estimated 50,000 people walked through the Parade of Homes and saw the evidence of Tim's faith.

"How can *I* accelerate toward my dreams?" you may ask. Hebrews 11:33 gives us the answer. Let's break it down:

"...who through faith..."

We know that faith, or a confident expectation and trust in God, is the starting point for everything. *Faith activates heaven to make what we believe a reality here on earth.*

"...conquered kingdoms..."

God has called and equipped you for conquest. You were made to engage the problem, not run from it. David ran *toward* Goliath. It's in the conquering, or facing the problem, that we find victory. *Your dream is on the other side of the battle!*

"...administered justice..."

By missing the key of administration, people lose money, time and resources. God told me, "My people are not occupying what I'm giving them." (Check out Exodus 23:28-30.) Whether it's taking care of your home, organizing your life, building your business or confronting problems head on, it's time to administrate the territory you already have.

This is who we are and what we can do through the power of God. It's never too late because God can accelerate you into your destiny!

Administrating Your Life

On a crisp September day the Lord told me to take another look at Hebrews 11:33, a scripture I was familiar with, because He wanted to show me something else. After a whole chapter of listing people who have done the impossible by tapping into the Kingdom, the writer simply says that he does not have the time to keep listing names and their stories. However, he does give us a hint. They all did it with this process: through faith they subdued kingdoms, administered righteousness and obtained the promises. This is the same process that we can walk out to enjoy the promises in our lives.

However, the Lord took me to the last part of that process, "administered justice," and said, "Here is where my people miss it." I did not know what He meant, so I kept praying and things began to make sense. "Justice" is what God calls right, or in other words it is "righteousness." It simply means putting things right that were wrong. We live in a world that is perverse and not operating according to God's righteousness. We must remember that we are the agents of God's government in the earth realm. We are to take dominion and exercise authority or administration here.

Enjoying the promises of God takes more than faith; it takes courage also. Courage is required to confront or engage the earth realm to bring about the change that righteousness declares. By faith we see what God has given us. But we must then act on that revelation for it to have any impact here. We engage the culture, the circumstances or the problems to see the change we need and want. However, once we overcome a situation, we need to know how to occupy our victory.

A lot of Christians get excited about the promises of God but do not have the courage to confront their situation.

And if they do confront their situation they still fail because they do not know how to occupy the place they were going. As an example, if a person was believing God for a business and they launched out by faith and did the things that were required to actually start their business (talking to the right people, securing the finances, developing a product, etc.), they could still fail! I have seen this so many times. They fail because they do not know how to run a business. Oh, they have the business, but they have no clue how to administrate it and it fails.

So in other words, we could have the store, declare how God brought it to pass, what a victory, but still fail because we did not know how to run a store, we did not know how to occupy our victory. This is rampant in the Body of Christ! Administration is something that we must either know or hire someone to do it in excellence. EVERYTHING has to be occupied or administered for us to enjoy the benefit of our dominion and inheritance.

Take time today and think about areas of your life that need organized, administrated better or given more attention. God can't give you more if you can't keep what you have. He will give you wisdom as to how to administrate the territory over which you are called.

Are You a Storm Chaser?

The other night, I was awakened by the crashes of thunder and the flashes of lightning outside my home. And it got me thinking, all of us can relate to going through some stormy situations in life. But it's in those storms that our courage and faith will shine. Satan loves to stomp around loudly, roaring like a lion, but let me tell you a secret: **HE HAS NO TEETH!** He can try to bring storms that seem threatening, but if you stand your ground, you can move the storms instead of allowing the storms to move you. Jesus did it when He and His disciples were out on the lake. All it took was one word from Jesus, and that storm shut up!

Here are a few things to remember during a storm, a kind of field guide to faith:

- Watch your words. Satan can't tell the difference between you and God when you are saying what God says. The same Power that created the universe is in you!

- Stay behind your shield of faith. It's only when you step out from behind that shield that Satan can see your human weakness.

- Stay in agreement with God. Satan is after your agreement with heaven. He wants you to let go of it. As long as you agree with God, those storms can't touch you. You may hear the thunder and see the lightning, but it can't come near you.

- Don't tell Satan you're afraid. Again, this comes back to words. Be brave, standing in the faith and strength of God and not your own. You may feel fear, just don't act on it. Satan sees that same anointing that was on Jesus—on YOU! Don't give away your feelings if they don't line up with heaven.

I believe in you, because the power of heaven is inside of you. I challenge you to stand unafraid in the face of storms. You are strong and fully able to overcome.

Are You Passing the Test?

Have you heard about Paul's "thorn in the flesh?" Did someone tell you that God did that to him? Well, let me tell you something that might shock you—God didn't give Paul this problem, and it wasn't about sickness.

See, Paul was receiving huge revelations and Satan hated it. So, Satan came immediately for the Word. The thorn in the flesh was an irritation that Paul kept coming up against. He was encountering resistance in his efforts to share the Gospel. And God couldn't remove it.

Satan has a legal right to test you. He doesn't know your heart, and he wants to make sure that you don't get into agreement with heaven—because He knows that the only way that heaven can invade earth is if earth comes into agreement. So, he attacks the agreement. He doesn't want that Word to produce, so he brings trouble and persecution to see if you're really in agreement. And most of the time he comes undercover.

But we've been given authority to trample him under our feet if we keep in agreement with heaven. If we step out of that, we don't have any ability to overcome. But if you resist him, James

4:7 tells us that he will flee from you. Picture that—the enemy running from you in terror.

Don't be ignorant of his schemes. He wants to steal, kill and destroy, but you're fully equipped to deal with him. Paul uses a Roman soldier as an example for us in Ephesians 6:11-18. He tells us how we can protect ourselves and overcome the enemy's advances:

> **Put on the full armor of God, so that you can take your stand against the devil's schemes. For our struggle is not against flesh and blood, but against the rulers, against the authorities, against the powers of this dark world and against the spiritual forces of evil in the heavenly realms. Therefore put on the full armor of God, so that when the day of evil comes, you may be able to stand your ground, and after you have done everything, to stand. Stand firm then, with the belt of truth buckled around your waist, with the breastplate of righteousness in place, and with your feet fitted with the readiness that comes from the gospel of peace. In addition to all this, take up the shield of faith, with which you can extinguish all the flaming arrows of the evil one. Take the helmet of salvation and the sword of the Spirit, which is the word of God. And pray in the Spirit on all occasions with all kinds of prayers and requests. With this in mind, be alert...!**

Satan is going to try to condemn you and make you feel bad. You have to have that breastplate so you can defend yourself with what Jesus has said about you, not what you've done, or what the enemy reminds you of.

Before I pastored, I woke up one morning and I was really sick. I went to the hospital, but the doctors couldn't find anything wrong with me. I really didn't know if I was going to live or die. I went

It's your turn now. You're supposed to be the light of the world. Philippians 2:14-16a tell us we should:

> **Do everything without grumbling or arguing, so that you may become blameless and pure, "children of God without fault in a warped and crooked generation." Then you will *shine among them like stars in the sky.***

You don't have to purpose to see the stars. You don't have to convince someone that there are stars. In the darkness of the night, stars stand out as points of light. Religion is like that—always trying to convince people that there are stars. People don't need to *see religion*. They need to *see light*. They need to *see* the *proof* of God in your life.

No one should have to ask you if you're a Christian. It should be obvious.

We were having a meeting in the Philippines several years ago, and a pastor who had been paralyzed and in the hospital for 40 days wanted to come. He hitched a ride in the back of a coconut truck for 12 hours. He couldn't come the first night because he was in so much pain. His friends made him go the second night and we prayed for him. He was *instantly* healed. The meeting changed drastically at that point. The crowd rushed forward and surrounded me. They were grabbing my hands and putting them on their heads. I finally realized they wanted me to pray for them. They had planned to have a meeting that evening to figure out how to pay for that pastor's bills and how to feed his family since he had been paralyzed from the stroke, but now they didn't have to. They realized that were seeing the real deal, and they wanted some for themselves.

See, when you have a demonstration of the Kingdom of God in your life, you don't need church potlucks, Bible studies and scripture memorization. Those things are all well and good, but the world could care less about our churches and our scriptures. They're out in the malls and restaurants living life. You have to be able to show them how your life is better.

> *God wants to elevate you to a platform of influence. Isaiah tells us that He will plant us in places where people will want to know why your life, your marriage, your family is different.*

Then, when people wonder how it's happening for you, you give them the Word of God. Otherwise, you're just bothering people. After all, the biblical model of sharing the love of God isn't about browbeating with scriptures.

We have to let the demonstration speak *for* us. In John 10, Jesus told the disciples that even if they didn't believe Him, they should believe the miracles— the *deeds*.

Second Peter 1:16 captures it perfectly. It says,

> **For we did not follow cleverly devised stories when we told you about the coming of our Lord Jesus Christ in power, but we were eyewitnesses of his majesty.**

That's all people want. They want to be an eyewitness to the glory of God. They want to know how you've been healed, how your marriage is no longer falling apart or how you got out of debt. You should be demonstrating results that are different than what the world normally sees.

God wants to elevate you to a platform of influence. Isaiah tells us that He will plant us in places where people will want to know why your life, your marriage, your family is different.

Stop thinking you're not much of an example. Remember you are a child of God. Our tendency as human beings is to look at the natural, to trust in the natural and to look at our past failures. But the Bible tells us that the promise comes by faith and it's guaranteed by grace. It's God's grace that does the work. It's not about you—it's about you and God. That's what the baptism of the Holy Spirit is all about. You shall receive power to *witness*, to be the *light*, to be the demonstration.

It just takes a willingness to step up and say, "I'll do that." People all around you have problems. They need God and God needs you. All you have to do is step into their lives for a second. You don't have to have it all together or even know what to say. God knows. All you have to do is be available.

> *It's God's grace that does the work. It's not about you—it's about you and God.*

It will take courage, so make a decision that you won't be intimidated. Remember that darkness is intimidated by light. Be about your Father's business. Be light, and watch what happens.

Are You the Bug or the Windshield?

It might be an old analogy, but it's a good one: Are you the bug or the windshield? Here's how you know.

You're the Bug if:

1. You're getting hit and smacked around by life.

2. You're stressed out and overwhelmed.

3. You have no hope.

4. You're waiting for the next hit.
   - Are you always worried about what will need repaired next, which kid will get in trouble next or how long before your husband loses "this" job?

5. You're just surviving.
   - Are you living paycheck to paycheck? Are you constantly worried about the next car payment, the next mortgage payment or how you're going to buy groceries next month?

6. You're living in the past.

7. You hang around with people who aren't driving their own car.

   o Are you letting the devil, your family or even your well-meaning Christian friends who are losing in life keep you in idle?

8. You're not dreaming anymore.

   o Do you wonder where the time has gone? Do you wonder what happened to the life you thought you were supposed to have? Are you self-medicating to escape today?

You're the Windshield if:

1. You know you have a God-given purpose. Even if you don't know exactly what it is yet, you know that God made you unique for a specific assignment.

2. When hard things come at you, you know that you are more than a conqueror. (Romans 8:37.) You're persevering; you can't be moved by the things that come against you.

3. You know you're not alone driving the car. You know that nothing can separate you from the love of God. (Romans 8:35-39.)

4. You have stories of going through "swarms of bugs" and them smashing against your windshield. (Luke 10:18-19.)

5. You're moving forward.

You don't have to be the bug. God is in you and He wants you to win in life. He has anointed you to drive someplace, but you've got to take the wheel and drive your life. You can't be passive. Be the windshield. Even if you're covered by the debris the enemy has been throwing at you as you tear through his territory, keep moving forward.

Be an Influencer to the Least of These

Do you know the best way for the enemy to affect our lives? Do you know the best place for him to start if he wants to corrupt or pervert our *entire* culture? It's with the *children*.

Yearly we host a Vacation Bible School program at Faith Life Church. I see so much energy and potential in the hundreds of children who attend each year. I see their eagerness to learn; they are like sponges, like blank pages. I am also reminded of how impressionable they are, that each of those children has a destiny and a calling, and that *we* are responsible for them.

Statistics show that we're not doing a good job. In fact, most surveys show that more than 50 percent of the kids today aren't serving Christ, and will not serve Christ. The church isn't doing a good job either. We're losing at least 50 percent of our young people, too—they aren't staying in church.

We know there is a problem and we have to ask why. My friend, David Sumrall and I shared this message together at my church. Here's some more of our message.

Did you know that when Hitler took over Germany he began with the youth core? It's true. He realized he had to capture the hearts of the youth to have the nation. We're seeing that in America now. No, I'm not being extreme. Just take a minute and really pay attention. Watch some cartoons. Look at the toys that are being marketed to kids. Research some of the video game content that is out there right now. Things that we might call innocent are not innocent at all. They're pushing the young people in this country farther away from the church and farther away from God.

But who's to blame? We can't blame the young people. We have to blame the parents. We're a generation of pleasure-seeking people. We don't understand what God has said about children, let alone His plan for them. So what do we do? How do we get an understanding? We look to the Bible.

Let's start with Abraham. What does Abraham have to do with raising children? Well, God said He wanted a godly seed from Abraham and He made Abraham some really big promises, but they were all contingent on one thing—he had to raise his family properly.

God created family and takes how we train our children very seriously. As a pastor I teach my people that all prosperity starts at home—first with your marriage and then with your family. When a man comes to me and says that things are not going well financially, the first question I ask him is, "How is your marriage going?" I have found that my whole life is going to hinge on how I live my life, not at church but at home. Everything good flows out of the family. Because of that, we need to realize that the promises of God for our life are still dependent on us following after God, mentoring and demonstrating righteousness (what God calls right), justice (what God says is legal) and His ways to our family. We have to teach our children to think, talk and act like God designed us to think, talk and act.

It grieves me when I hear parents tell their kids that they are brats or that they wish the summer school vacation was over so the kids would be out of their hair. Children are precious, gifts from the Lord. The Bible also tells us that children are a reward—that they are like arrows in the hand of a warrior. Think about that. How vital is an arrow to a warrior? How much care and protection does he give to his arrows because he knows his life depends on them? How well is that warrior going to protect and oversee the value and the condition of his arrows?

Do we pay as much attention to young people today as a warrior would to his arrows? Are we nurturing and raising those arrows up straight—with a righteous mindset and a spiritual worldview?

Okay, I get it, you say, but what can we really do to influence young people for God? Well, in order for us to be an example for anyone, and to be the person that our kids would want to grow up to be, we have to look at what's going on inside of *us*. Kids are not stupid, they watch you and they will follow what you do instead of what you say. If you have a heart for God, they will know it. My kids are all serving God and in the ministry. I never demanded that my kids ever go to church; they always begged to go. They love God because they have seen too much. They have seen our lives change financially, have seen countless people healed before their eyes and know that God is good. Where else would they want to go? So make a decision that for you and your house, you will serve the Lord.

Be the person God has called you to be, and your kids will want to be like you. Other young people will want to be like you. Remember that where the young people go, the nation will follow.

Do You Know What Time It Is?

On a trip to Armenia we traveled through Paris. While we were there, we walked down to the Eiffel Tower and saw a display they had about the World's Fair held there in 1900. It was an amazing event. About 56 million visitors went to that fair that year and watched as things like talking film, moving sidewalks and diesel fuel made their debuts. People were excited to be there. They were excited to see these new inventions on the brink of changing the world.

They were looking forward, but they had no idea what was ahead. Fourteen years later, WWI broke out. One million French men were killed. It was the most devastating conflict in human history.

We can't see what's ahead either, but God has provided us with some information. In Matthew 24:37, Jesus is teaching about the end times. He compares it to the times of Noah, when the people didn't have a clue. They didn't know why they were on the earth or what they were supposed to be doing, so they were going about their daily lives until the flood came and swept them away.

Jesus also talks about it in Matthew 16:

> **He replied, "When evening comes, you say, 'It will be fair weather, for the sky is red,' and in the morning, 'Today it will be stormy, for the sky is red and overcast.' You know how to interpret the appearance of the sky, but you cannot interpret the signs of the times. A wicked and adulterous generation looks for a sign, but none will be given it except the sign of Jonah." Jesus then left them and went away.**

What Jesus was saying was that an adulterous, wicked generation is callous to the truth. He was talking about our hearts. See, we can interpret the weather, but not the times. We have to see the times for what they are. We have to get a proper perspective.

It's harvest season now. We've got work to do.

In Proverb 6:6, you see a proper perspective of time. Now, this addresses those that are lazy, and I'm not aiming at that. I'm looking at the process. Proverb 6 says to look at the ant. It has no commander, but it recognizes the seasons and urgency of the moment. The ant has a proper perspective of time. We need a proper perspective of the times and what life is all about also.

In John 4:32, after a long day of ministry, Jesus' disciples offer Him something to eat and He declines. Jesus tells the disciples that He had food to eat that they did not know of. The disciples were confused, but Jesus went on to say that the food He was speaking of was "to do the will of him who sent me." Jesus had a proper perspective of the urgency of the hour. He told them to open their eyes and see that the fields were ripe and the harvest was now!

He knew that harvest season is a race against time. You have to stop what you're doing and go after the harvest. .

It's harvest season now. We've got work to do.

You have yesterdays, and you have tomorrows, but you can only live in today. Anything you want to change about your life has to change today. Do you have a proper understanding of who you are and whose you are? Do you know why you're here? Or are you wasting your life on things that make no difference?

People are dying *today*. People need fed *today*. People need help *today*. It's time to be about the Father's business. Don't wait until the end of your life to get a proper perspective.

Lift your eyes now. The clock is ticking.

Don't Leave Your Assignment

1 Corinthians 3:10a

By the grace God has given me, I laid a foundation as an expert builder." *Master Builder"* #

One of the most important principles that you will ever learn is that you have a specific function and assignment, and that is where the grace of God is found. As Paul say, he laid a foundation as an expert builder—according to the grace that was given him. When God gives you an assignment, He gives you the grace for it. *Grace* means *God's empowerment.*

For instance, when you get married, you have the grace to be a husband or wife. Whatever God calls you to do, the grace is there to accomplish it. But the grace of God is accessed by faith. If we draw back in fear, there is no grace for that. One of the things I tell my church is to always say yes to God and figure it out later. Sometimes if you try to figure things out, if you can do what you sense God is leading you to do, you will leave God's grace out of the equation. God's grace can only be accessed by faith and following Him.

Drenda and I have done things that scared me spitless. The only way I could face the mountains God called me to face was just by saying "yes," closing my eyes and following His Spirit. If I weighed my ability against the assignment, I was sunk. As I said yes to God an interesting thing happened, however. My ability increased and I actually began to enjoy what God had called me to do.

> *Perseverance is needed to finish our assignments and reap the harvest and reward of the assignment.*

Another mistake people make is quitting after they start on a God assignment. Once we start out on the journey, many times we then realize how hard it really is to push through. Perseverance is needed to finish our assignments and reap the harvest and reward of the assignment. Every assignment that God gives us has profit in it, both for God and us. The enemy will try to get us discouraged to the point of quitting at times. But we can lean on that grace of God and make it through to completion. Drenda and I always say we have done everything naïvely—we just stepped out. Although we have faced some tough times, we have found God faithful to His Word. We have so many supernatural manifestations of finances, healings, divine direction and wisdom that our confidence has grown over the years. Now God can trust us with bigger and bigger assignments.

Let me sum up what I am trying to say—don't quit!!!

Ears to Hear

Have you ever wondered why Jesus spoke in parables?

In Matthew 13:11 Jesus said, "And He replied to them, To you it has been given to know the secrets and mysteries of the Kingdom of heaven, but to them it has not been given" (AMP).

See, we have our Bible stories, but they're not just Bible stories. Hidden in those stories are mysteries that can bring revelation to us about how the Kingdom of God operates, but we must have ears to hear. When we talk about ears, we mean your spirit. These mysteries are meant for you. You're not supposed to just stumble along and hope things will work out. You're supposed to advance!

But we forget we're in a battle. We don't take the spiritual adversary we have seriously. We've been watching TV and cartoons all of our lives, and we downplay him to just some guy with horns and a red cape. But Satan is alive and demons are real, and they don't want to see you prosper and advance in God's mission for your life. This is the reason the Bible says Jesus spoke everything in parables—to keep things from the enemy.

Think about it. The adversary would love to cut you off at the pass. God prevents that by keeping things hidden until the right time.

When we first started our TV ministry, our bills were big. Every month we were watching $50,000 - $70,000 go out the door. It was really tough. When you're not used to spending that kind of money, it can get pretty unnerving. And that's where I was. So, one day I was praying. I'll call it that, but I was really complaining. I was telling God how there just wasn't enough money in the account and that this was a really tough spot to be in. He listened for a few minutes and then He rebuked me. He said, "Is it due today?"

See, one of the weapons of our warfare is timing—spiritual timing. We don't understand it, but God does. So, He shows up at the midnight hour. He waits until the last second so that the enemy can't bring interference and hold things up. Because if Satan understands the plan of God, he will change tactics to intercept it. He'll bring pressure, trouble and persecution against us. He'll do everything he can to stop it.

Think of it like a really great spy movie. That's how God does things. He moves behind the scenes with people that don't look like the "right" people. Look at me—I was the poster child for debt. But God delights in using people like me. Or people like David.

David came into the camp and saw Goliath ranting and raving. Saul offered David his armor, but David wouldn't take it. He ran out to the battle line with only his staff and his sling. Yep—the Bible actually says he ran toward Goliath. Goliath was taken off guard. The tactic worked and David killed him.

God's going to use unusual ways to advance His cause right under the nose of the enemy. Psalm 23 says God delights in preparing a table for you in the presence of your enemy. He loves that. We do, too. God wants to use you like that, but you have to have ears to hear.

In 2 Corinthians 11, Paul talks about his escape from a king. Look at it. The walls were all shut up. There was no way to escape. Paul was in a situation where they were going to take his life. It was impossible for him to escape, but God made a way. Paul was let down in a basket through a small window in the wall. Now, I want you to underline this next part. Underline where Paul says, "…and I escaped through his fingers" (AMP).

This is what your life should sound like as you follow God! If you have ears to hear, your life will be spent slipping through the enemy's hands and advancing the cause of God with your life.

Many times in the New Testament, it's recorded that people wanted to stone Jesus, but that He slipped through the enemy's hands. In the end, Jesus' life wasn't taken—He laid it down.

The thing you have to get used to, though, is the intimidation of the event. It's not easy to wait until the midnight hour. It's not easy to not know where the money is coming from or how in the world you're going to defeat a giant. It's not easy to listen to the enemy howling at you. But, if you have ears to hear, you'll know the tactic before it comes. You'll have a way of escape. God will make sure that you slip through the cracks. But you have to be confident in being able to hear and letting the Holy Spirit lead you. Unusual and amazing things will happen when you have ears to hear.

Why did Jesus tell Peter to catch a fish? I'm sure they probably had enough money to pay their temple tax, but Jesus was a teacher. He had to teach them how this thing operated. He knew He was only going to be there for a limited amount of time, so He taught them.

How unusual do you think it was to catch a fish with money in its mouth? Jesus was teaching Peter to take unusual instructions. See, the enemy knows your weaknesses. When God gives you instructions, He's going to give you an unusual strategy in order to protect His plan. Jesus was training Peter to get accustomed to unusual instructions. Granted, He had him catch a fish. Peter knew how to catch fish and the enemy knew Peter knew how to catch fish. So it wasn't a big deal. As far as the enemy was concerned, Peter was going about his normal day. But God was using an unusual tactic. And Jesus said the first fish. Peter had to be obedient to instruction. We have to be obedient to instruction, too.

God knows where things are. He knows where your provision is. It's not going to come in the typical way you think it will come or the enemy will set himself against it, and prevent it from happening.

The enemy walks in darkness. He doesn't know the plan of God. But when you receive direction from God and you take that first step toward it, the anointing increases and he picks up on that. He also picks up on words and tries to figure out what's happening. Don't sit around telling friends and family the vision God has given you. It's not too hard for the enemy to pick up on that. And don't procrastinate or be disobedient! Had Peter searched through the mouths of 50 fish, Satan would've picked up on those fish and brought interference and tried to intercept what God was wanting to do there.

We need to have ears to hear the strategy for our lives. Now, you can train yourself to discern these things. You have to do that. Practice it. It's your weapon. As you follow these things in your life, your life will sound better than any novel you've ever read. It will read like the Book of Acts—full of close calls and what looked like the end when, out of nowhere, God comes through—again and again. I have so many stories like this, personally, that I could go on and on with examples, but I just don't have enough room here.

I really want you to get this. Stop folding up every time the enemy bluffs you or tries to deceive you! Take the time to get these mysteries so you can stand your ground and really build something. To many people the Bible is just stories, but when you're born again, it's full of revelation. Ask God to reveal the mysteries and you'll see that the next time you study you'll say, "Wait a minute! Has that really been there all along?" He'll give you a glimpse of your destiny. If you will have ears to hear, submit and walk it out, you're going to have stories just like Jesus, like David and like I do.

Evidence

Job. This book of the Bible is used all the time to explain away—to justify—the things people are dealing with. After all, it's much easier to say that God is allowing something to happen to us than to say that God is trying to get something corrected in our lives.

Think about it. Why would God want to purposely put His people through things just for kicks? That isn't what the world needs to see, and God is trying to reach the world. He knows people need to see something different. You don't need religion, do you? You don't need to just see nice buildings, right? You need the reality of the Gospel. You need to know that God is alive and that you can trust Him with your problems. You need proof. You need evidence.

The Bible talks about this. Jesus talked about it. Look at John 3. Nicodemus saw the miraculous signs that followed Jesus. He saw the evidence. He went to Jesus and pretty much said, "We know you can do the things you do because God is with you." Everything that Jesus was doing validated who He said He was. In John 14:11 He even said, "Believe Me for the sake of the [very] works themselves" (AMP).

And in Matthew 11 when John the Baptist sent two of his disciples to find out about Jesus, Jesus told them to go back and tell John what they had HEARD and SEEN—the evidence. What was it? The signs—the demonstration—of the Kingdom of God.

In Acts 8, verse 6 tells us that multitudes of people paid close attention to what Phillip had to say because they heard and saw the miracles he performed in Jesus' name.

So what's our evidence? Since we can't see Jesus or the disciples performing miracles, what do we look for? We look for a demonstration of the Kingdom of God.

Take Monica's story, for example. In January 2007, Monica had a chest infection that took an ugly turn. It triggered an immune response and began to attack her nerves. She began to have numbness. Then her body began to shut down. She couldn't swallow. She couldn't move. She was paralyzed.

But Monica believed God. She knew of other stories of healing. She knew what the Bible said. She had her evidence. She believed she had the victory. She rebuked everything that didn't line up with the Word of God. She believed she would walk again and she pushed herself to recuperate. Now, Monica is healthy and now her story is evidence.

A few years ago a man just happened to be driving by while he was in town and he came to our church. We didn't know him, but during that service we had a word of knowledge that someone had a problem with his or her left leg and foot. When we asked who that person was, this man came up for prayer. We prayed for him and he told us about himself. He said that his lower leg and foot had been numb for almost four years. Well, the next week he came back again smiling. He said that when we prayed nothing seemed to happen. But when he woke up in the morning, his foot was completely normal—he could feel everything. At the end of service he came up again for prayer, asking for healing for his same foot. I was a little confused but he went on to explain that now that he could feel his foot he realized that he had a callus on the bottom of his foot that was causing some discomfort when he walked. So we prayed for that as well.

I thought it was a rather funny story but it illustrates what I am saying. This man had seen what God could do and was basically saying, "Hey, I want all of it, let's not leave any part that is not healed." Once you see the evidence of the Kingdom of God, you will be hooked for life and say, "Let's not leave any part out, I'll take it all!"

T.L. Osborn, founder of Osborn Ministries, wrote in his book *Healing the Sick* that, in the early years of his ministry, he struggled with giving people evidence that the Bible was the true Word of God, especially when he was confronted with other religions overseas. But one night Jesus walked into his bedroom and spoke to him about his ministry. After that life-changing experience with Jesus, T.L. operated out of complete confidence. Osborn Ministries has since had one of the greatest 50 years of ministry ever recorded.

Miraculous stories like Monica's, or the man visiting our church, or that of T.L. Osborn's are what validate that we are of Christ. These signs follow those that believe. So if we all believe in Jesus, why don't we all have these signs following us? Because we haven't been taught that. In your normal Christian experience this isn't normal. "Even to hear these kind of stories may be strange to you." To even think it's possible is requiring you to drastically change your thinking. You haven't heard of people with cancerous tumors being healed and people that were paralyzed getting up and walking away before. But you are now. We're changing your perception of what it means to be Christ-like—what it means to share the Gospel.

Now, how do you get the evidence? How do you share it? Well, we all know that you can't heal someone on your own—only God can. And God heals through the Holy Spirit. See, when you are baptized in the Holy Spirit, it's like a coat—a God coat. You've put God on and you're carrying Him with you wherever you go, just like Jesus did. If you look at your Bible, you'll see that there is no recorded time before Jesus was baptized in the Holy Spirit that He was able to perform miracles. Jesus needed God. We need God. We need the Holy Spirit.

I grew up in a very conservative, denominational church. I still thank God for that church, but while I was there, I didn't hear about the Holy Spirit or about miracles. I was hungry for God. I kept reading the book of Acts and wondering why those things had stopped. One day an evangelist came through my dad's pizza shop where I was working and talked to me. He told me about the power of the Holy Spirit and I was thrilled. He said Jesus is still doing the same things He did in the Bible. He told me he was preaching a revival and that I should come down and hear what he had to say. So I went and I was hooked on the presence of God.

It was there at that church that I met three ladies who were talking about the Holy Spirit and a morning Bible study they held in their home. Working in the small town pizza shop, I had met these ladies as they picked up pizza in my store. I asked them if I could attend, and they gladly said yes. They began to teach me about the Baptism of the Holy Spirit and invited me to attend a big citywide rally, which I attended. It was there I received the Baptism of the Holy Spirit for myself.

Back at my church I was the youth leader, and I couldn't wait to share what I had found out about the Baptism of the Holy Spirit.

I went to our little youth meeting and told the youth group about it and asked those who wanted it to raise their hands. Then I prayed and was amazed as the 15 or so kids in that meeting began to cry, laugh or shake—they were all glowing and many speaking in tongues.

Now, there is much more to this story, but let me skip to the end. The next week at Sunday service, I was sitting toward the back of the church when during the quiet moment of meditation one of those kids got up and tapped me on the shoulder and said, "Let's go." I was confused as to what he was doing up and walking during that most sacred moment in the service. He could see that I was confused and he then went on to say he wanted to go and pray for his mom who was up on the second row. I remembered that his mother was facing some severe back issues and was going in for surgery to have five disks fused together, a serious operation and disability.

So I walked up front with him, thinking that he would just simply quietly pray for his mother, but I was shocked when he picked his mother up and carried her to the front of the church and began to pray for her in tongues as loud as he could. Now, mind you, my pastor didn't agree with tongues. In fact, he had told me they were of the devil.

But that didn't matter. This guy prayed for his mother in tongues and she was instantly healed. She never had the surgery they were telling her was required. The anointing gave the evidence of God. That would not have happened without the Baptism of the Holy Spirit.

The signs follow them that believe. That hasn't changed. The signs point to Jesus. As we allow the Holy Spirit to work through us, He validates who Jesus is and points to Him. This EVIDENCE can do more in one moment than you can do in 20 years of preaching or trying to coerce someone to believe your God. You simply have to be brave enough and courageous enough to let Him use you.

We don't need any more religious talk. We don't need to have any more lengthy conversations to try and convince people of God. What they want to see is validation of God's Kingdom and the evidence that He cares for them.

So, are you willing to risk being a fool? Are you willing to step out in the name of the Lord? Will you validate the Gospel? Will you bring the evidence? Will you be the evidence? You need equipped with that power, the Baptism of the Holy Spirit. This Baptism is for everyone to have and to walk in today. The power of God has not passed away but is here for today, just as it was then; and it is available to you—just say YES to it!

Acts 2:38-39

> **Peter replied, "Repent and be baptized, every one of you in the name of Jesus Christ for the forgiveness of your sins. And you will receive the gift of the Holy Spirit. The promise is for you and your children and for all who are far off—for all whom the Lord our God will call."**

Face the Mess

One day I caught an episode of a television program about hoarders. The family was living with roaches. They were not setting off bug bombs or calling exterminators to come in and spray, but living with them, almost like they were pets. It was broad daylight and there were roaches in their sink, in their dishwasher and in their refrigerator. Yes, I said their refrigerator.

The mother was the hoarder and the teen kids and husband were living with it, and with the roaches. I couldn't watch anymore. Maybe you've seen that program and maybe you haven't. For whatever reason, the people and families who are on that program can't deal with the mess. Some of them cause it; some of them are content living with it; some are overwhelmed by it. In every case, they can't see how to deal with it. But we watch it and we think we know how to deal with it. We say, "Well, I know what I would do." Or we say we'd never even let it get that bad in the first place, right?

See, it's easy to see that problem from our perspective. We're not in the mess. Our perception may be that it's easy to fix. Just grab some trash bags. Clean it. Burn it. Whatever. But what we don't realize is that every one of us has a mess to which we've grown accustomed. Sure, it probably isn't roaches in the refrigerator, but we all have something. And from God's perspective, our messes are pretty simple to deal with, too. Imagine if you had God's perspective on your mess. You could clean it up pretty fast, right?

God wants you to be free. He wants you to win. He wants to change your perspective on life. Too many believers say they're living for God, but they're not taking dominion or occupying their life. Is that you? Are you living with a mess that hurts your life and steals your dreams and visions? By putting up with it, you reveal that you don't know who you are.

Because God determined the day you were born. He had a plan for your life and the time in which you would live. In Acts 17:26, Paul tells us:

From one man he made all the nations, that they should inhabit the whole earth; and he marked out their appointed times in history and the boundaries of their lands.

You have to get God's perspective. He made you unique for a special purpose. He doesn't do things by happenstance. He has a very clear purpose for everything He does, and He has a very clear purpose for your life.

So diagnose yourself. (Brace yourself. I'm going there.)

Answer these questions:

- What are you thinking about all day?

- Are you focused, or are your days a blur?

- Are you on Facebook and Twitter all day?

- Do you waste hours watching television, or focusing on a hobby that isn't going to amount to anything?

- How clean is your car? Are there French fries smashed between the seats?

- Do your neighbors drive by your house wondering why you haven't taken care of the weeds?

- Does your babysitter show up every day wondering why you never wash those dishes?

And how about spiritual messes?

- Are you jealous of someone else?

- Are you envious of the life someone else is living?

- Are you holding onto unforgiveness or any other mess?

It's not much fun to face the messes in our lives. It takes some time to clean out the stuff from under the bed, in the closet and in the garage. But you have to face it and clean it up, or nothing is going to change.

You have to shine God's light on it. That's when you'll have revelation of who you are, and you'll wonder why you've put up with it for so long.

God made you and He wants to help you. He will lead you and guide you. He wants to lead you with His grace to face the mess. Not to discourage you, but to change your perception.

So, deal with the situation that's in front of you. Deal with the issues. Get on the scale. Pull out the bill drawer. Stop kidding yourself.

Clean your car up and you might find that you really like your car. Clean your house and it might actually feel like a retreat. Clean your life up and you might realize it's a pretty good life after all.

Don't wait until next week, or two weeks or the New Year to start. Spend some time with God now and get His perspective.

He'll help you face the mess.

God is Good

Let me tell you about a newsletter I recently received from a ministry.

In it is the story of Jim and his father. Jim's father had been an alcoholic for 30 years. Jim, his wife and his mother had continued to pray for his father, but with no apparent result. Jim's father refused to admit he had a problem with alcohol and refused to hear anything about God. The newsletter says that one day Jim, the son, heard this minister speak about the power that is released when we begin to praise God for everything in our lives instead of pleading with Him to change it. So Jim went to his wife and said, "Honey, let us thank God for Dad's alcoholism and praise the Lord that it is part of His wonderful plan for Dad's life."

Do you see anything wrong with this so far? Let me keep going.

The author goes on to say that to praise God is to express our acceptance of something God is permitting to happen, so to praise God for difficult situations like sickness or disaster means, literally, that we accept it's happening as part of God's plan to reveal His perfect love to us.

Okay. Come on. Do you see the problem with this? It just keeps getting worse. In fact, he goes on to say, "The very fact that we praise God and not some unknown fate also means that we are accepting the fact that God is responsible for what is happening and will always make it work for our good."

I'm turning myself loose on that. I got so mad reading this stuff. Really—is that supposed to encourage you? So, let's thank God for the cancer. Let's thank Him that it's His perfect will for our lives and that He's demonstrating His love for us. I mean, if God be against me, who can be for me, right? No!

Let's look at a scripture they quoted in this newsletter—Romans 8:28. "And we know that in all things God works for the good of those who love him, who have been called according to his purpose."

Just be sure you know that God is good—all the time!

It says, "IN all things." We don't thank Him FOR all things. That's the most ludicrous thing I've ever heard in my life. The encouragement of this scripture is that in all things God is working for our good, that He is working to move that situation to a positive outcome. If I am sick, God is working for my healing. If I am in a tough spot, God is working to bring me wisdom to deal with it. You get my point. The Bible says, "Do not be deceived." God is good all the time. He's only good. The Bible says every good and perfect gift comes from God. He doesn't change. In fact, that's how you recognize what to resist. The thief comes to steal, kill and destroy—not God. We don't thank God for bad things. But this is the kind of stuff that's out there. This is what religious leaders are teaching.

Now, don't get me wrong. The Bible does say we shouldn't

be anxious for anything. So, there is a principle of praising God and thanking God, but we don't want to thank Him for what the devil is doing. Acts 10:38 says Jesus went around doing good and healing all who were oppressed of the devil. The devil oppresses, not God. This stuff makes me mad.

So be sure that you are firmly anchored to the love of God and that you know that God is good. The most common statement I hear is "God allowed this" or "God allowed that." Did He really? Well, we need to be sure we know God so we can say, "The devil brought this and the devil brought that, and we can resist him in the faith and stand our ground on what is right and not be deceived."

Just be sure you know that God is good—all the time!

Amen & Amen!

Find Your Fragments

John 6:12

Gather the fragments that are left over. Let nothing be wasted.

Years ago, I discovered that the average family could be out of debt, including their home mortgage, in less than 7 years. When I discovered this truth I couldn't believe it. In fact, I worked over dozens of my clients' files to verify my theory. After a few weeks of fact checking, I was convinced. Then I had another thought. Why doesn't everyone know this? Why are people paying mortgages for 30 years when they could be out of debt in 7 years? So, I took my facts to my clients and asked them this question. They answered that they never even thought it was possible.

So, I developed a company around my discovery, and that company has been producing for dozens of years for my family and helping thousands of families—families that didn't know it was possible. What we have to realize is that there are many institutions, and people, that simply don't want families to discover these truths because their income depends on people's ignorance. This is exactly how the devil works as well. He's convinced us that there's no chance of winning in life, having success, paying off our houses, etc. Most people just don't think it's possible. But, in life, knowledge is a powerful weapon. Think about it. Most people think that finances are too hard to understand. Whenever something is "too hard to understand," it's a perfect spot for an ambush. The devil—and greedy men—will set you up for loss *every* time. Ignorance costs us a lot.

As we begin to ask the Lord for direction in the area of finances, many times He will have us look inward first—at the possible losses that we can capture and reposition to pay off debt. I call this the power of a fragment—those seemingly insignificant pieces that, by themselves, seem small but, when put together, add up to a sizable amount that can have a tremendous impact on your financial future. When I work with families in their finances, I look at everything they are doing with their money. I take the time to help them identify areas that can be changed. Those are usually areas that they never thought of. In the same way, the Holy Spirit will help you by pointing out areas that you need to change. You see, when we ask the Holy Spirit to help us, He takes it seriously. But, be forewarned, *everything* is up for review when you ask God to help!

Pray and ask the Lord to help you by pointing out things that can be changed in your current lifestyle—ways that you are being wasteful. Jesus did this when the disciples fed the 5,000 men in Mark 6. The disciples didn't even consider picking up the fragments because they only saw them as scraps. But Jesus said, "Gather the fragments and let nothing be wasted." That's what God is saying to you! Let Him point out areas that you never thought of that are just waiting to be captured. Any normal person finds it very exciting to find lost money. The Kingdom works the same way! We get to discover just how great our inheritance and our futures are as we work with God. It's an amazing journey!

Five Ways to Find Your Function in Life

I was in a church one time when this big bus rolled in with a band's name on the side. I thought I was going to be witnessing some great concert, but I was wrong. The band was awful. They couldn't sing. In fact, it was one of the worst noises I have ever heard in my life. This band had spent all of this money on instruments, and on this bus, when they could have better used that money somewhere else. It was like watching *American Idol* tryouts. Have you ever wondered where these people's friends are? Why hasn't anyone told them? Where are their moms? Why didn't someone tell them they couldn't sing?

That's how silly it looks for us to try to do something that we're not gifted for. We can try to move in directions and do things because we think that's where the money is, because we think it's cool or popular or because that's where we think the glory is, but we just end up embarrassing ourselves if we try to function as something other than what God has designed us for.

The dictionary defines "function" as "an activity or purpose natural to or intended for a person or thing; a practical use or purpose in design."

Look at a cup. It has a very defined function. It's made to be a cup. If I try to use it for something else, it isn't going to be effective. We have people all over the Body of Christ who are trying to be something other than the cups they were called to be, but they're not effective. We have to find our fit—our specific purpose and function.

Paul talks about function in 1 Corinthians 12. He's reminding the church that the Body is ONE unit, and he's teaching them about the importance of functioning that way. In verse 15, he says, "If the foot should say, 'Because I am not an eye, I am not of the body,' is it therefore not of the body?" See, the devil will lie to you if you don't understand proper function. He'll tell you you're not important, that you're not valuable. He'll tell you there isn't glory in what you're doing because you can't sing, or you're not on the platform or at the forefront, but that's a lie. You can think you're insignificant, but the whole Body has been arranged just as God wanted it to be. That inferiority was happening in Corinth. Paul was correcting that. He was also correcting the people on the other side—the prideful ones.

We all know someone who has "spiritual dreams" every night. You know, the person who wants to tell you all about how God tells them what color shirt to wear, what color socks to wear, all of it. Why do people do that? Because they have spiritual pride. See, pride says, "Look at me! Look at all my spiritual gifts! I don't need you! I hear God for myself." But that's a very dangerous road to go down. That road will take you right out of here. You can't get your identity by being more spiritual than others. People like that think they have a spiritual mind, but Paul says the opposite. He says they have lost connection with the head—with Jesus Christ. You don't want to follow anyone like that. People were looking down on each other in the church and Paul was correcting that, because those parts of the Body that seem to be weaker are indispensable. God has orchestrated the function of every person in the Body no matter how small.

Ask any leader what the most valuable giftings are in their church and they're likely to say helps and administrations. Those aren't the people in the forefront or on the platform, but everything would crumble in five seconds without those vital people—those vital functions.

Instead of clamoring for attention, being jealous of each other, trying to posture ourselves as being more important and following after the people we think have the most anointing, we should be functioning in unity. We should be edifying others and building them up. We should be loving people and honoring God. That's why chapters 12, 13 and 14 of 1 Corinthians flow together. Paul dives right in there. He wants us to recognize the significance of every function.

We're all going to stand before Christ someday and tell what we did with our assignment. Someone is depending on your function. How will you answer when you're asked how you used it?

The people you thought were so eloquent and spiritual may just be in the back, while some little, old lady who quietly interceded at her house every day will be at the front because she was faithful over that call, that assignment, that function.

So, no more rock star mentalities. We're in this together. Find your function and add value to the whole Body.

So, how do you find your function? Here are FIVE ways:

1.   What bothers you? What problems do you want to fix? Others might not see the same things you see because that's your function. See a wall with a dent in it? Grab a paintbrush. Become the answer.

2.   What brings you the greatest satisfaction? In the earth-curse system, we made all of our decisions based on money. We had to do what was asked of us in order to make money. Because of that, people don't really know what brings them true satisfaction. So, experiment. Try some things. Find out what brings you satisfaction.

3.   Start doing something. It's hard to evaluate something from a standstill. Jump in somewhere.

4.   Remember to own the vision, not the position. A small church starts up and they need a musician. After some time, a lady finally speaks up and says she took about six months of piano lessons, so they give her the job. Eventually, the church grows, and a "more seasoned" piano player is put in her position. But that lady with the six months of lessons gets offended when they ask her to do something else. Don't be her. Don't get offended. Be willing to be moved around. Own the vision, not the position.

5.   Volunteer. If you won't do it for free, why should you get paid to do it? Most of our staff began as volunteers. God is going to promote you. He's going to help the leaders see that you should be promoted. Get involved.

Fixing Your Faith

Have you ever felt desperate? Have you ever needed God to do something, and needed Him to do it quickly? We've all been there—in those situations where faith has to produce, where God has to show up.

Several years ago, I knew a family who hit a deer and totaled one of their two cars. Then, two weeks later, the other car had the engine blow. That's not a good place to be, right? So, they decided that they were going to believe God not to use debt to replace those vehicles, but the clock was ticking. They had a rental car, but it wouldn't be for long. So, the day before the rental car had to be turned in, they got a phone call from a friend who didn't know what had happened. That friend wanted to know if they knew of anyone who needed a car. When they explained what had happened to them, the friend gave them the car.

That encouraged them, so they decided to believe God for a van that would fit their entire family. They really wanted a Honda Odyssey, so they came into agreement as a family and released their faith for it. A few weeks after that, we stopped by their house and on their refrigerator was a big picture of a Honda Odyssey. Each time they opened the refrigerator they would lay their hands on that picture and thank God for that van.

About a week later, my secretary called me and said, "We had an unusual call this morning. Someone called and said they want to give the church a van." Of course, she didn't know what this family was believing God for, so I asked her, "What kind of van is it?" And, you can guess the rest of the story, a Honda Odyssey. That van was actually in really good condition. When my wife called the woman to share the news, she first asked her how they were doing with the car situation. The woman said, "We're one day closer."

Now, I don't believe that was a coincidence. I know better. I've experienced the promises of God, and heard too many stories of the Kingdom operating in people's lives. In fact, I believe that it's critical that we learn how the Kingdom of God operates.

In Luke 8:43, we read about the woman who was healed after touching Jesus' cloak. This story illustrates a vital part of how the Kingdom of God operates. Jesus called the woman "daughter." That meant she had a legal right to the covenant—she had a legal right to be healed. It wasn't Jesus' faith that caused her to be healed. It was her faith that caused her to be healed. She was fully persuaded that God was going to do what He said He was going to do—that's faith.

For faith to exist, you must be fully persuaded that God is going to do what He said He would do. You have to get it in your heart. God needs you to be in agreement with heaven—in your heart. You can't beg hard enough, cry hard enough, fast hard enough, be good enough, read the Bible more times to prove you have faith. He needs your heart. Your mind may agree with it, you may be able to quote the scripture, but what do you believe in your heart? You have to get it in your heart to be fully persuaded.

See, God has to have someone in the earth realm who will come into agreement with heaven and carry the anointing. And your heart is the interface for that agreement. When you are fully persuaded in your heart, and you pray, the anointing flows. Without that agreement, prayer is just a religious exercise.

Now, once you get it in your heart, that doesn't necessarily mean that things are going to change right at that moment. There are things that need to be done. There's more to it than just having faith. You weren't saved just by faith, but by doing also. We can have faith, but there are some things we have to do in order for your picture to match what's in heaven:

1. You have to believe God.

2. You have to have direction from God.

3. You have to take action on that direction.

The woman with the issue of blood believed God. She saw Jesus right in front of her and she took action. Sometimes we believe our heart is right, so we step out in faith and we take action and nothing happens. Then we get frustrated, disillusioned and disappointed with God's Word because we're not seeing the results that the Bible clearly says are legally ours. But that's a great place to be.

Find the malfunction. Drill down until you figure out where you've missed it.

I know. You're thinking—this guy is nuts! How could he say that's a great place to be? Because frustration is the breeding ground of change. Have you ever built something that ended up not working? Ever stood back and looked at something you did and said, "Wait a minute. Something is wrong here?" You got frustrated, right? Then you went back to the instructions you never bothered to read in the first place and you start dissecting everything, and you realize you have a screw in the wrong place, a wire disconnected and that you need batteries. When you finally fix the issues, and get it in alignment, it works just like it was supposed to.

The BIBLE is just like that. It's supposed to work just like it says. If there's a malfunction, it is NEVER on God's end.

So, now you know. If you're there at the place of frustration, disappointment or desperation, you have some changes to make. Think about what you really believe. Find the malfunction. Drill down until you figure out where you've missed it. Go back to the Word of God and make sure your heart is right. Read the instruction manual and make sure you have the right picture on the inside. Then, go after the picture as hard as you can. Watch the changes that take place. Watch the stories show up. Watch the mountains move.

Freaked OUT!

During service I was teaching, I pulled out a rifle and aimed it at my son. Well, not exactly. I had a pellet rifle and my son, Tom, was about 100 feet away from me and he was holding a balloon. I asked him to hold the balloon at the side of his face. Then I pulled the trigger and freaked out everyone in the audience.

But the audience didn't have all the facts. See, there was no pellet in the gun. Tom had a little pin in his hand that he used to pop the balloon when I pulled the trigger. So to them, it LOOKED like I had shot the gun. We had effectively set the stage. We evoked emotions. We got a reaction.

That's exactly what the enemy does. He sets up a scheme, a scenario, to play you like a fiddle if you don't know the truth.

The Bible says in Hebrews 2:7-8 that God put everything under our dominion. God had crowned Adam with glory and honor, and he ruled in the earth realm under delegated authority. Think of it like a sheriff who stops a semi-truck. The driver of the truck pulls over because the sheriff has delegated authority. He has a government that backs him up. Adam had delegated authority until he sinned. Then he gave his crown away to Satan. But God sent Jesus—a man—to restore the delegated authority. So, now if God is going to do something in the earth realm, He has to do it through those that have authority here. He can't send angels, and Satan can't send demons. Both Kingdoms have to use men to do things.

Satan uses a lot of tactics to trick us out of our dominion. In Genesis 3 we see how crafty he really is. He tried to twist the character of God right out of the gate. He said, "Did God really say you must not eat of any of the trees in the Garden?" If Eve hadn't known the truth, she would have been deceived right away, but she wasn't. So, Satan changed his tactics. See, he has to get you to a place of agreement because faith is simply your heart being in agreement with heaven. And, just like faith is agreement with heaven, Satan has to get you in agreement, too.

And he's pretty sly. He takes a little bit of the principle of God, a little bit of the Word of God, and twists it. He uses it to deceive. But, if we know the truth, we can discern for ourselves. The only way to know the truth is to know the Word of God. That's how Jesus won His battle with Satan—He defended Himself with truth—with the Word of God.

Satan knows that faith is the currency of the Kingdom of heaven. He knows that if your heart holds onto the Word, it's going to produce. He also knows that it's imperishable and it's always going to produce after its own kind. Guess what? He doesn't like that. He claims this place as his. So, he has tactics he uses to get the Word out of your heart. The Parable of the Sower in Matthew 13 tells us some of them—trouble, persecution, stirring up strife, conflict—to get you to let go of the Word. He's going to try to do something, anything, and he's going to make it LOOK bigger than the Word.

But you can't freak out. You have to stay in faith (agreement) with what heaven says about you, about your situation and about the Kingdom of God. First Peter 5:8 tells us to be self-controlled and alert because our enemy prowls around like a roaring lion looking for someone to devour. When he sets that stage, our natural instinct is to react, to panic, to yield to fear, to let go of the Word, but God tells us not to let go no matter what is happening. We have to stay self-controlled. Yes, the enemy is going to roar. The Bible says he is like a roaring lion looking for someone to devour. That roar affects our perception. We focus on that roar and we forget who we are. We forget the promises of God. We forget what the Word says about our situation. We forget the enemy HAS NO TEETH.

> *You stand on the Word. You constantly speak it. Because the Word of God does not fail. God does not lie. Satan is defeated.*

Look at Matthew 17. A man brought his son to the disciples to cast out a demon. The son had seizures and foamed at the mouth, and the disciples got freaked out. Now, Jesus had just given them authority to cast out demons a few chapters earlier, but they couldn't cast this one out. So Jesus came and looked at what happened—the spirit started acting up again. Jesus was able to cast the demon out, so why couldn't the disciples do it? Because there was no agreement between heaven and earth. The disciples heard the roar and they got spooked. The devil LOOKED bigger than them. But Jesus knew the truth. He had agreement with heaven, He knew who He was and the authority He had.

A few months ago, baby Holland was born and had some complications. She went into cardiac arrest and had no heartbeat for 32 minutes.

Now, what you do in a situation like that determines life and death. How you respond, what you speak, what you come into agreement with determines the outcome. We were NOT agreeing with that outcome. We started speaking what God says. After 32 minutes, her heart started beating and went back to a normal heart rate. But you know what happened next—the enemy roared some more. "Oh, no. She had no oxygen for 32 minutes," "She's going to have brain damage," "Her arm jerked when she slept; she's having a seizure." Now, please don't misunderstand, but doctors aren't the final authority. Her parents were fighting the roars with the truth—they were believing for total healing. Baby Holland just recently had her final brain scan and you know what? Her brain is completely, 100 percent normal.

So, when the devil roars and you have the emotion rise up, or you're tempted to react, how should you deal with it? What do you do when he says things to you, when he tries to pull you into emotional discourse, or he reminds you where you blew it?

You fight back with the Word. You don't freak out. You stand on the Word. You constantly speak it. Because the Word of God does not fail. God does not lie. Satan is defeated.

The Bible tells us in Ephesians 6:10 to be strong in the Lord and His mighty power. Put on the full armor of God so that you can take your stand against the devil's schemes. Stay in agreement with what heaven said about your situation, and stay self-controlled. You don't have to buy into the roar when you know the truth.

Freedom–
It's Your Choice

If I asked you to give me one word that describes the United States of America, what would it be? It should be "FREEDOM."

Yes, I know America has problems, but in my opinion it's still the greatest country in the world. We are a blessed people. We can pick what we want. We can pick what we do. We can dream of our futures. We are free.

We talk about the problems we have in America, but you don't hear stories about people fighting or boarding ships to get into other countries, but they do that to get into the United States of America.

It's the freedom they want.

See, this great country was established with a government that gave people a right to express themselves freely, to create with unlimited potential. The founders of this great nation designed it based on freedom, which they believed was God's right for man. The concepts and ideas they used to build America were based on the Bible.

And we've created. Boy, have we created. Americans have

invented and produced some amazing things—the telephone, the artificial heart, the sewing machine, computers, the Internet, zippers, tractors, the radio, hearing aids, air conditioning, the Polio vaccine, lasers, CDs, microwave ovens, space shuttles. The list goes on and on. We talk about other nations, but there has never been a people and a nation as productive as the U.S.

We are free to create, dream dreams and impact the world.

Of course nations aren't born freely. People gave their lives for the birth of the United States of America. We honor our veterans and servicemen and women on Memorial Day. To date, about 1.4 million men and women have given their lives in the defense of the U.S.A. They went before us. They gave us the chance to be free today.

And, we're still free, but now we have a problem. We're at a crossroads. America is in a crisis. What makes America great is being lost. We have a heart problem. We've developed an entitlement mentality. In the depression, people traveled the country looking for a job. Today, people travel to the nearest government office looking for a handout. People now look at the government as their answer. In fact, we have 60 percent of our adult population receiving some sort of government assistance each month. Not all of that is bad, but I'm referring to a mindset. We've grown to depend on other people instead of ourselves. We've come to depend on government instead of God.

America wasn't founded that way. She was founded on the beliefs that you could produce your own future, you could own your future, you could build it as big as you wanted to and you could change your family's future.

We have to go back to this—to what is right. We have to speak up. The government isn't our problem. It's our thinking. We have to change the way we think. It's the only way that America will survive.

So, if you have been lackadaisical, repent. Change your thinking. Remember that people have given their lives for your freedom. Don't take it for granted. Show your appreciation by passing it on.

And get prepared for the fight ahead. Help educate those younger than you. Remind them of the price of liberty. Teach them that freedom has a price. Demonstrate righteousness. Rally around what made this country great.

2 Chronicles 7:14

> **If my people, who are called by my name, will humble themselves and pray and seek my face and turn from their wicked ways, then I will hear from heaven, and I will forgive their sin and will heal their land.**

Freedom From Poverty

As I shared, my wife, Drenda and I started our life in debt even though we were Christians. We went to church and heard the Pastor say that God will meet our needs, and we believed it but did not really know how to walk it out when circumstances waged a war with our minds. Somehow we ended up going backwards to the verge of bankruptcy. Finally in despair, I came to the startling conclusion that something was wrong and it wasn't God, it was me.

I began a quest to understand the Word of God and the Kingdom. God began to teach me these things that I had overlooked before, and we were faithful to stick with the process. As we walked these things out, we paid off all the debt and became free financially. Let me tell you, that was a great day. Let me say it again. Seeing the Kingdom of God work just like the Bible said it would was absolutely thrilling!

In Luke, the fifth chapter there is a story about some fishermen, self-employed businessmen who were facing some bad times. They had done all the right things, had the right supplies and spared no expense in preparing for business, but after fishing all night they found themselves with empty nets. They had done all they could do yet it was not enough.

Does this sound familiar to you? Do you know anyone who has worked hard but has still had to face failure as the end result?

These were seasoned fishermen who knew how, where and when to fish, yet they came up empty handed. When Peter lent Jesus his boat, which in itself represented the fishing business, it CHANGED KINGDOMS. Once the boats had been brought under the jurisdiction of the Kingdom of God, God could then legally bring provision to it. In this case, the result was that the nets and the boats were filled so they could not hold anymore. This is a great example of the hundred-fold return. Many people think that the hundred-fold return is a multiplying factor of what they give, for instance let's say a hundred times what we sow. This is incorrect; the hundred-fold return is the measure with which you have given being returned to you, pressed down, shaken together and running over. (Luke 6:38.) Peter's business was the measure he gave to God, and that's the measure that was filled to overflowing.

> *When Peter lent Jesus his boat, which in itself represented the fishing business, it CHANGED KINGDOMS.*

Proverb 10:22 says, "The blessing of the Lord brings wealth, and he adds no trouble to it."

Proverb 10:22 works! God brings wealth and He adds no sorrow with it. This same Kingdom is the Kingdom that you are part of if you are born again. This same potential is already yours! Your failure can turn to success just by making a few changes in how you operate and to which kingdom you lean for your provision.

Get
the Advantage

We've all done it. We've thought about "authority" and immediately felt uncomfortable or even fearful. Maybe the word "authority" reminds you of how your heart races when you pass a police officer after you've been speeding. Or maybe it makes you think about how you couldn't eat before you made that big presentation in front of your boss and his bosses last week. Or maybe the word "authority" has always been represented by the face of a certain teacher from childhood that you'd really rather forget.

Whatever we think the reason is behind our fear or dislike of authority, the truth is that we feel that way because we've been out of line. We haven't always respected authority or realized the role God has assigned to the authorities in our lives.

Our culture has taught us to use phrases like "It's all about me," "You deserve it" and "Have it your way." Our lives have become focused on our feelings, our agendas and our survival. Unfortunately this "orphan mentality" is resulting in a culture that doesn't acknowledge, let alone respect, authority. The Bible warns us of this. We have to stop dismissing this mentality as innocent. It's not. The scriptures tell us that all authority is from

God. His Kingdom is our example, and it operates by the power of authority—a Kingdom with a King.

> *Do your very best with the responsibilities you've been given. Be flexible and servant-minded. Stop worrying about titles. Don't try to claim territory. Ask how you can help. Humbly ask for advice. Stop getting offended. Propel yourself by connecting.*

So why has God placed authorities in our lives? How do we benefit from respecting and honoring authorities? Besides the obvious reasons, the Bible tells us that learning how to operate properly under authority gives us an advantage. What is the advantage? The results of mentorship.

The world defines a mentor as an experienced and trusted advisor, but I believe God has mentorship in mind every time He puts someone in a position of authority or leadership. By submitting to and obeying those "mentors," with respect and sincerity of heart just as we would Christ, we posture ourselves to receive from God. He puts us under the leadership of people who have something He knows we need, and when those "mentors" step into the role God has called them to they provide:

- Correction when our attitudes or actions are wrong.

- Rebuke when we're making mistakes or not heeding quickly enough.

- Encouragement when we do well.

- Careful instruction on how to walk life out.

- Help in producing good fruit and character.

So look at where God has placed you. Figure out what leader He has assigned you to and serve them. If you already have a mentor, ask yourself, "When they think of me do they have joy? Would they trust me enough to put me in charge of all of the affairs of their estate?" If both of those answers are not "yes" then you have some work to do.

Let God use people to train you so you can win. Learn all you can. Do your very best with the responsibilities you've been given. Be flexible and servant-minded. Stop worrying about titles. Don't try to claim territory. Ask how you can help. Humbly ask for advice. Stop getting offended. Propel yourself by connecting. Learn the lesson now so life won't have to teach it to you later. Become someone's answer and get your promotion.

This kind of teaching never generates a big "hooray" from our culture but it is vital in God's Kingdom.

Get Unsettled

I think that Christians get confused sometimes. We look for things to be easy. But God never said things would be easy; He just said all things are possible.

See, the way you're living life right now has capped your ability to expand and move on. You're living, right now, at your current level of capacity, and for that to change, you must change. To test my theory let me explain what a capped capacity feels like—being overwhelmed. If you are struggling to do more in a day then you are capped. People who are capped stop dreaming; they are consumed by all the daily details of keeping up. People who have a capped capacity are maxed out. To unleash further progress you must increase your capacity by changing the processes in which you handle your current responsibilities. For instance, a farmer may have to buy a second combine to keep up with harvest if he wants more acreage to farm. A businessperson may have to hire more help to get the job done. But all of this can be summed up with one word—change.

Change isn't pleasant. Change deals with weakness. We have to deal with ourselves. We have to deal with our weaknesses, the circumstances and other people, and quite frankly, it's not necessarily easy. A lot of people don't have the courage for change, or the fortitude for it, simply because they don't understand the reward of it. Change is going to be uncomfortable. There's going to be some chaos involved.

You're going to have to get unsettled with yourself, and you're going to have to be unsettled with your circumstances. You've got to begin to say, "Well, you know, why do I live with that? Why do I put up with this?" So, change will be unsettling. Because **success is a series of uncomfortable decisions.**

Uncomfortable, tough decisions are required for success. It WILL get worse before it gets better. Look at the Israelites. God had a specific destiny for them. He sent them out of the land of slavery into a land flowing with milk and honey, a place that He created for them to live in, dwell in and occupy.

They had an assignment and a purpose. So do you. You have a place that God is leading you to. All the events of your life, the way you have been created, your thinking, your creativity, your personality—all of it was designed by God for your destiny. You're on the road to that place. You have to recognize the place, but most Christians miss their destiny because they stay at the Red Sea experience.

The Red Sea experience is when you're born again and you celebrate your new freedom in Christ, but then you stop. You stop and say, "Hey, praise God, brother. How are you doing? I'm doing great! It's awesome we're saved."

But WHY are you saved? And why are you still here? If being saved was just about going to heaven, then why are you still here? There must be a reason. There must be a place God has destined you to dwell, a place of occupation where He wants His government represented.

After the Red Sea came the Jordan River. The same Spirit of God that blasted apart the Red Sea blasted the Jordan River apart. Why? It wasn't for deliverance this time. It was for conquest, territory and occupation!

So, for the believer that thinks that everything is supposed to be easy, you better blow that theology out of the water! God is trying to push you into the land of giants and walled cities! He's saying, "Here you go! Bam!"

The water parts and there you are, by faith, taking it on. You long for your own land. You long for your destiny. That's the promise, but it comes by faith.

So, where are you called to be? Where are you created to dwell? What needs to change for you to get there?

Getting the Process Started

I love to hear people's stories. I love to hear how people's lives have been changed, their bodies have been healed, their marriages and families have been made whole and their finances have been fixed.

Testimonies give you a picture of hope. You can listen to someone's story and know that that can happen for you, too. And, although faith isn't produced by a story, it does aim you at Jesus.

I'm excited to be at a church that has those kinds of stories on a regular basis. In fact, we have too much evidence. Just recently, for example, Sarah Traylor shared her story.

When Sarah was two years old, she had an asthma attack. She turned blue. When she was officially diagnosed with asthma at age five, she began a regular regimen that included breathing masks and inhalers. She carried inhalers with her everywhere she went. She had one in her purse, next to her bed and in her car.

Random things would trigger an attack. Sarah couldn't be exposed to cold air or run the vacuum because of the dust. She couldn't even drink a thick milkshake. And she absolutely couldn't miss a dose of her inhaler medication. She had been hospitalized more times than she could count. Her mom, a nurse, even said that, as a child, it was easier to just take her with her to work at night in the ER than to get a phone call from her dad that she couldn't breathe.

Sarah had been on medication nearly thirty years. A few weeks before she shared her story, that all changed.

Sarah heard my daughter's story of being healed from a massive tumor. Doctors told Amy that the mass in her abdomen was just the way her body was formed; they did not see the massive tumor. Because the doctors were not alarmed Amy began to accept her situation as normal until one day the Holy Spirit prompted her to fight and demand that her body be normal. Amy asked the elders to pray with her, and a week later Amy woke up to find that she had lost thirteen pounds and nine inches around her waist while she slept, instantly healed. Amy's testimony hit Sarah so hard she couldn't speak—she had done just what Amy had done—she had accepted what the doctors had said was normal for her. She repented for trusting and believing what the doctors had said over what God had said. She received her healing right there in her chair, and, from that day forward, she hasn't had to take her inhaler or use any medication.

In the pocket in her purse where her inhaler used to be, Sarah now carries a piece of paper full of healing scriptures. Why is that important? Because when you're healed you have to fight for it. You have to believe God. You have to do things like carry scriptures around so that, when you don't feel like you're healed, you can remind yourself, and the enemy, of what God has said.

We have to find out what the Word of God says about our situation, and we have to stand on it. We have to speak only what God has said about our situation.

Look at the story of Joshua with me.

Joshua had been mentored by Moses, and Moses had died. So here Joshua was taking over this huge nation of people—millions of people. He was responsible for them through this wilderness journey. It was a big job.

What did God say about Joshua? He told Joshua that He would give them every place they set their foot. Then He said that no one would be able to stand against Joshua all the days of his life. Then, God said—listen to this—"I will never leave you nor forsake you."

Now, Joshua could have looked at his situation and said, "You've got to be kidding me, Lord." He could have looked at the millions of people surrounding him and said, "You want me to do what with these grumblers? With all the problems Moses had? This is impossible!"

But he didn't.

Joshua heard God say that He was with him and to "Be strong and courageous." In fact, God went on to command it when He said, "I have COMMANDED you to be strong and courageous."

God said that because He knew Joshua was going to be tempted to be terrified and discouraged. He reassured Joshua that he wasn't alone. He basically said, "Hey, it's not just you here. It's you and me. I have promised never to go anywhere. We're going to get this job done." The task that was set before Joshua was impossible without God. The task that is set before you is impossible without God. In order to make it possible, you're going to have to do a few things.

First, you're going to have to take your eyes off of who you think you are and set them on who God says you are. Abraham was called by God to leave his family, his hometown—everything—because he was promised something that wasn't even possible in the natural. He was past the age of bearing children, and he willingly gave up everything to walk out the promise. God told Abraham to lift up his eyes, and Abraham obeyed.

That's the first thing you must do—lift your eyes up from where you are. See what God says about your future and where you are to be.

We have a tendency as human beings to pay attention to the details around us, or to what was behind us, but you can't go someplace new if you aren't looking forward. So, where do we look? To God! Let Him show you who you really are and who He has made you to be. Look to Him and His Word and let Him affirm you.

Then, you're going to have to hear what God says and walk it out. Because, more than likely—like Joshua and Abraham—you're going to be called to go someplace you've never been before. They had to walk it out. So will you.

Let Him show you who you really are and who He has made you to be. Look to Him and His Word and let Him affirm you.

You have to know that God has promised to be with you, to give you the direction you need and to make it happen with you, no matter what problems may arise. Because God loves when the odds are stacked against Him. That's when He shines. You don't need God if you're going to walk in the possible. You don't need Him if you're going to play it safe, and never venture outside of your comfort zone.

But if you want a life full of stories, victories and conquests —things you want to pass on to your grandkids—you must learn to be uncomfortable. But know that God is faithful. He has a plan. He's not caught off guard or taken by surprise. He knows all the details, and He has the answer.

So, train yourself to hear His voice, to think like He thinks and to know His good and perfect will. And, when He tells you something, WRITE IT DOWN! Take ownership of it. Say, "That's mine!" There'll be pressure against it, but you can defend the position because you know what God has said to you.

Then—stand! Stay the course. Don't quit. Don't throw in the towel. Stay focused. Don't panic. Guard your heart. Meditate on the Word day and night. Say what God says. Make the Word life to you. Don't try to do it without God's help.

After all, He's promised never to leave you nor forsake you.

And, if God is for you, who can be against you?

Go Ahead, Make God's Day!

Psalm 35:27

Let the Lord be magnified, Who takes pleasure in the prosperity of His servant. (AMP)

So many people get in heated debates about whether or not God wants to prosper them. I can't believe how many Christians talk about all the hardships that God brought to them: death, disease, bankruptcy— that one minister even credited God with making a man an alcoholic! I certainly wouldn't want any of these "Christians" as my Public Relations agent! We are God's ambassadors. We're His P.R. agents. What people see in your life and mine is a direct representation to them of God and His goodness or, in these people's case, the negative outcome of knowing God. That's the problem. These people probably mean well, but they don't KNOW God, His ways or His Word.

Throughout the Word of God we see that if someone understood God and His covenant, and was obedient to His commands, they were blessed. No wonder God actually delights in the prosperity of His servants! He wants the world to see, "If you follow Father God, it's going to be a wonderful life." The Israelites are a great example of this. They didn't have the better covenant that we have, but even when they obeyed they lived in peace and prosperity. Every time the Israelites "did evil in the sight of God" they went into slavery and bondage and missed the blessing of God for their lives. That hasn't changed today.

People perish for lack of knowledge—knowledge that God is good and He does good things for His children. He blesses them and delights to prosper them. The mark of a good father is the way he takes care of his children. We understand this in natural parenting. If a man gave his children cancer or tempted them to do evil, or relinquished them to a life of alcoholism, we would call that man a child abuser. Our God says, "If you being evil men know how to give good gifts to your children, how much more will God give good gifts to His children?" (Matthew 7:11.) If it brings pleasure to our Father to give you prosperity, then why don't you make God's day and prosper?

I really mean that. People are watching you, and your decision to persevere with the Word of God may make the difference in someone making it to heaven! They may decide based on the evidence in your life that God really has answers and they should turn and follow Him. It will open doors that give you an opportunity to impact the Kingdom of God. Ultimately, it will make Him joyful! Isn't that what the word "pleasure" means? Its definition is a high degree of enjoyment or delight; joy; rapture. I love thinking that God gets overjoyed with rapture when good things are coming into my life because I have tapped into His Kingdom laws through obedience and faith. Religion has misconstrued this true picture of God. But you know as a parent how wonderful it feels to see your children blessed, and how painful it is when they are misguided and experience bondage as a result.

It's time we brought God a high degree of enjoyment! He can't make us prosperous without our consent, belief and obedience to follow His ways. Just like you want to bless your children when they obey, God desires to prosper you! We must follow the precepts in His Word to receive. If we won't, He can't!

Make a decision to believe that you are God's child, and realize that He gets pleasure from you and your life when you're blessed. Weed your heart of any wrong teaching, and guard your spirit from teaching that perverts the image of God's character.

Go ahead and make God's day!

Have You Been Baited?

I received an email recently that said, "To be quite honest, Gary, I'm not sure how much longer I can keep doing this. I know God is guiding me and He is directing me, but this sowing thing just isn't working. Can you help?"

I get questions like this all the time. And I've been telling people why it isn't working for them. In fact, I just wrapped up the series *Fixing Your Faith: What to Do When It Doesn't Seem to Be Working*. In the last message, I talked about the number one way we cut ourselves off from the Kingdom—OFFENSE.

Look at Mark 11. We read verses 22-24 all the time and we talk about faith. But we don't look at verse 25 very often. "And when you stand praying, if you hold anything against anyone, forgive them, so that your Father in heaven may forgive you your sins."

Why did Jesus put that in there? What did that have to do with faith or the fig tree dying? Why did He say that?

Look at Romans 13:8-10.

> **Let no debt remain outstanding, except the continuing debt to love one another, for whoever loves others has**

fulfilled the law. The commandments, "You shall not commit adultery," "You shall not murder," "You shall not steal," "You shall not covet," and whatever other command there may be, are summed up in this one command: "Love your neighbor as yourself." Love does no harm to a neighbor. Therefore love is the fulfillment of the law.

Love is the fulfillment of the law. So, we're expected to love others as we love ourselves. If we step out of that—out of love— it's exactly the same thing as committing adultery or murder as far as the Kingdom is concerned. Because the Law of Love governs us. So, you can say you follow the Ten Commandments, but do you LOVE?

See, Satan doesn't have to tempt you to murder someone. He doesn't have to tempt you to steal. He just has to tempt you to come outside of love and you've stepped outside of God's legal jurisdiction. That's why 1 Peter 3 says that husbands need to walk in love with their wives or they will hinder their prayers. Satan comes against marriage because he knows that, if he can get you divided and outside of love, then the whole thing shuts down.

Of course the enemy is going to try to bait you outside of your love walk, and He's going to use people. There will be people who try to cause turmoil or conflict in your life. Someone will cut you off in traffic. Your kid will tell you you're mean. Your husband will say he doesn't like your haircut. Your neighbors will forget to invite you to their party.

We have the potential to pick up an offense every single day of our lives. The enemy will do whatever he can to pull you out of love, out of peace. None of us are exempt.

When we began to pastor, we had plenty of turmoil and plenty of people who started acting up. One day, I was backing out of a driveway, and I saw a bicyclist coming down the hill in the distance. Apparently, he was closer than he appeared, or going faster than I estimated, because when I backed out there he was. And, let me tell you, he was angry. I hadn't hit him, but he decided he was going to hit me. He took his bike and kept beating it against my car, and using words that weren't appropriate and showing me his finger puppets. And I got offended. Then, I thought I'd teach him a lesson.

The devil will set you up. I made a little plan to ambush this guy. I backed into a driveway down the road and waited for him. Then I did something my wife can tell you that I have really never done in all the years we've been married—I rolled my window down and spoke his language for a few minutes. Then I hit the gas and grazed that bicycle, and I was so proud of myself. Then I heard a voice on the inside of me yell, "GARY! WHAT ARE YOU DOING? The guy obviously isn't born again. YOU'RE A PASTOR!" I had blown it.

Yes, I tried to find the guy. Yes, I felt guilty. But I had felt justified. That's how we are. We have this mindset that the offenses and the attitudes we have are a personal thing and that we're justified. We can explain what that person did to us, why we don't like them or how awful they've been, but in a spiritual court of law, we'll lose.

In Matthew 18:21-35 we see the Parable of the Unmerciful Servant—read it. You're that person that has all that debt forgiven. You're that person and you have zero justification not to forgive someone else. If you don't do that, you're incurring judgment. You're separating yourself from God.

Just like the Unmerciful Servant, when you fail to forgive someone, you're pronouncing judgment and condemnation over him or her. It doesn't matter how many promises of God you can quote, if you're judging and condemning, you're outside of love. If you're outside of love, you've cut off the Kingdom.

I really hope you get this. It's truly life and death. If the Kingdom isn't working, there's always a reason. The most effective way the enemy pulls us out of the Kingdom is with offenses. And he's going to keep trying. He's going to set up schemes and people to pull you out of love, and he's going to try to use you to offend others. It's his greatest mission. He even tried it with Jesus. Yet, in the midst of the greatest betrayal, Jesus still taught love and forgiveness, and gave Himself for it.

So, judge yourself. Humble yourself. Let the Holy Spirit discipline you. Ask God to help you to be that quick to forgive. Overlook all offenses. Then, you'll really see the Kingdom of God operating in your life.

Healing: God's Plan

I'm going there. I'm stepping right into the controversy. People might get offended, but I'm still going to talk about it. You need to really get this and hold onto it with everything you've got.

I talk about it because I know what my Bible says. I know Jesus already paid the price for me to have it. I've experienced it—healing.

It's a touchy subject. It may be difficult for you, too. Maybe you know someone who didn't receive their healing or someone who can quote scripture after scripture about healing, but it just hasn't happened for them. Maybe that's you. Can you believe in healing for other people, but you just can't seem to get ahold of it for yourself? I've been there, friend. I've been sick to the place where I didn't know if I was going to live or die. And that's where God taught me some things, and I want to share those things with you.

So let's start by looking at where sickness and disease come from. Would you say, "From the enemy?" Sickness can be a result of the dominion of the enemy in the earth realm, but every sickness is not from the devil. Sometimes it's our fault. We might be doing something to affect our health. Maybe you're eating something you shouldn't be eating or you're not getting enough rest. Or maybe there is sin in your life that you haven't addressed.

"Now, wait just a minute, Gary," you say, "what does sin have to do with my back pain, or anything else I'm dealing with?" There are ways that we open the door for the enemy to affect our lives. One of those ways is through sin. And if we look at what Jesus said—specifically in Luke 5—we see it firsthand. What did Jesus say when He saw the guy lowered through the roof? He said, "Friend, your sins are forgiven." And He got some grief for it. Why did He say that? Because Jesus knew that sin gives sickness a legal entrance into our lives. He knew that sin cuts us off from the power of God and without the power we can't get the promises—and healing is a promise.

You know it's in there—look at your Bible. God told the nation of Israel that if they did what was right before Him that He would not bring any of the diseases on them that He brought on the Egyptians. Ephesians tells us that the same power—to heal—that was in Jesus lives in us. We see in Psalms that He sent His Word and healed them—that He rescued them from the grave. Acts tells us that Jesus went around healing ALL. The promise of healing is everywhere in the Word of God.

But there is one scripture that undeniably proves our legal right to healing—Isaiah 53:5—by His wounds, His stripes, we are healed. You see, Jesus already paid the price. He paid for our healing. He bore it all so that we don't have to.

So many Christians say, "I believe that God is going to heal me," or "I'm waiting on God to heal me," but they've got it wrong. Jesus already paid for our healing. You don't become healed. You were healed—2,000 years ago. Faith is not coming. Faith will not be. Faith IS. It is the substance of things hoped for and the evidence of things not seen.

And this is where things get difficult. This is where you really have to deal with yourself. Our natural mind wants to see, but we know faith is the evidence of things not seen. We have to get this—the Word of God has the power to bring to pass what it says, and when we have faith for what the Word says, we enact a spiritual law that brings it into existence. We will not see until we have faith when we can't see it.

That was a revelation to me. I was that person who thought I was waiting on God. I had the right concept, but I hadn't crossed over into faith. I shared my story earlier. Drenda and I had a hard time with money for a very long time. It produced a lot of fear in me. I was always putting out fires and trying to survive. It wreaked havoc with my emotions and I was very high-strung. I had some issues come up with my body. I woke up one morning and I was numb—my face, my hands, my legs, even my tongue—and it scared me. I started having panic attacks and heart palpitations. They put me on drugs and the drugs made it worse. Something was going on with my body that they couldn't explain and I was scared. I wanted to see my kids grow up, so I did the only thing I had left to do—I began to search out the Word like never before.

I would get up and study the Word. I wanted to know what the Bible said about healing. God had to teach me. When we heard of a healing conference in Tulsa, we went, and I went up for prayer. The anointing was very strong and I was out for about 30 minutes. When Drenda came down and touched me, she was out, too—it was a very strong anointing. But something wasn't right. When I walked out of the building that night I still felt sick and I asked God why. I dreamt that night a scripture, which Drenda told me the next morning was Mark 11:24.

All of a sudden a light bulb went off. I got it. The Word of God told me I was healed but I wasn't acting like it. I would say, "Okay,

I'm healed," then "No, I guess I'm not," or "I'm waiting for my healing." But I was already healed. I had to walk my faith out.

So what did I do? I headed to Weber's Root Beer Stand. See, before if I ever ate sugar or anything with carbohydrates in it, I would begin to shake and almost go into a coma. I was actually afraid to eat anything with carbs in it. After God spoke to me, I decided to walk it out. I drank two large mugs that day.

Now, maybe you're not there yet. Maybe you're not ready to walk it out. Maybe you need to make things right with God first. Have you made Him Lord of your life? Are you far away from Him? Stop trying to carry it out in your own strength. Stop trying to break away from it on your own. Call on Jesus. Give Him everything. Don't try to face the problems by yourself.

Do you have some work to do? Ask God if you're the problem. Read healing scriptures and write them down. Get just one that you can anchor your faith to and read it—out loud—constantly. Find someone who has faith to pray for you—someone that believes what the Bible says about healing, who says, "Yes. It's God covenant—it's your legal right—to be healed. You can resist sickness. You don't have to take it!"

Then stop accepting every diagnosis and the names that doctors give you and the prophecies they tell you about diseases in your body—the Word of God supersedes all of it.

Believe the Word. Say what the Word says. Say yes to the covenant. Say yes to God. Thank Him that you have the right to be healed. Now walk in that right.

Healing: What Does the Bible Say?

Health is a big deal. Right now, people are arguing about it. It's all over the news. Everyone is talking about it these days, even our government. Why is that?

Because health issues cost money. Because they rob us of the life we want to have.

So, have you talked to your family about healthcare? Do you know what they think about it? What about your friends? Where do they stand on the important issues? How about your church? What do those people think? And, how about your elected officials? What are they saying?

If you know all of those views, you've got it covered, right? Well, wait just a minute.

Can you tell me what the Bible says about it?

I told you that healing is a promise from God. I gave you a few specific places in the Bible for reference. I shared Isaiah 53:5—by His wounds, His stripes, we are healed. But there is more. There is so much more.

So go get your Bible. We have a lot of work to do. Go on and get it.

You have to have your Bible with you because this is warfare and your Bible is your weapon. Sickness and disease are spiritual battles. When you're fighting those battles you have to know your legal rights. You have to know what the Bible says. You can't try to fight just knowing what I say or what the TV preacher says. You have to know the Bible for yourself.

Let's begin by looking at Matthew 8:16. It says in my Bible that Jesus restored to health ALL who were sick. What does your Bible say?

How about Matthew 4:23? What does that say? Matthew 9:35? Matthew 12:15? Matthew 14:14? Matthew 15:30? Matthew 19:2? Matthew 21:14? Acts 10:38? I could keep going.

But that's Jesus, you say. Of course He healed everyone. Well, look at Luke 9:1. Jesus gave the disciples the same power He had to heal people. Now look at Luke 9:6, then Luke 10:1-9. This is where Jesus appointed 70 others to carry on the mission of preaching the Gospel and healing people.

In Mark 16:15-18 we read that Jesus authorized and deputized the church to do the exact same thing. He said if we believe and are baptized that we have His power, His Spirit, and that we're to go out and lay hands on the sick so that they will get well.

You see, the promise of healing is everywhere in the Word of God.

What's the deal then? Why are some people healed and others are not? Well, read this:

In 1997, Tracy started going numb in her toes. She was afraid.

The numbness would start in her toes and would travel up her body. She compared it to having a stroke. It would strike the right side of her body, and she wouldn't be able to walk or use her body properly. She couldn't even brush her hair. That went on for three years. Then she was diagnosed with Multiple Sclerosis.

Tracy knew she needed God. She went to her mom's church for prayer, but then her mom told her she needed to find Jesus for herself and Tracy listened. She says she sat on her bed and started reading her Bible from the beginning. Then, Tracy found what she was looking for. She saw that Jesus had healed all of our diseases and that the word "healed" was past tense.

But Tracy says she was still really dealing with symptoms—symptoms so bad that she felt her life was being stolen from her. She says she kept on asking God to heal her, begging Him and trying to be good in order to get healed, but it wasn't working. Then in 2007 a friend told her that she should watch what she was saying out of her mouth and to find more teaching on healing. At that point Tracy really started getting it. She realized that God is not a liar—He's a healer—and even though she was still dealing with symptoms, she was already healed. Now, for the past two years, Tracy has been walking in health. She received her healing.

Notice something—Tracy wasn't trying to get healed. She had revelation that she was already healed, but what was the catch? She had to enforce it. She had to start saying out of her mouth that God had healed her, regardless of what people might have said to her or what it might have looked like.

So what is the difference between Tracy and someone who hasn't received their healing?

Tracy found out what the Bible said. She became confident when she began to study the Word of God. She learned what is legal and not legal according to God. Then she began to enforce it.

One critical thing that prevents us from receiving our healing is our lack of confidence. When you're not sure what you believe, you're not confident. People are not confident that it's God will to heal because they don't know the Word. We have to know beyond a shadow of a doubt that it's God's will to heal every time or we can't possibly be confident. We've been taught that God allows sickness, that He uses it to teach people things or that He'll heal when He's ready to heal, and we've lost confidence. None of that is scripture—none of that is the will of God.

Once you know the will of God you can know that justice will be served for you. The only way you know the will of God is to study the Word of God.

Another thing that prevents us from receiving our healing is tradition. The Bible says in Matthew 15:6 that tradition nullifies the Word of God. What is tradition? It's the passing on of beliefs or customs from generation to generation. How many times have you heard, "I don't believe like that," or "My church doesn't teach that?" Who cares what your church says? Who cares what I say? You need to know what the Bible says about it!

What has been set up in your mind about yourself? What have you learned or possibly adapted to that does not line up with God's Word?

Let's change it. Let's change your mentality. Let's stop saying, "Help me" and start saying, "Let's find out what God's will is." Let's get to where you're thanking God that you've already been helped.

How do we do that? Get in the Word of God. Guard your heart and make sure you're putting faith in there. Put faith and the Word of God in your heart before anything comes into your life. Because sometimes you don't have time to get your Bible, and you need to be prepared. Have the Word of God in your heart so you can get to it if you can't get to your Bible. Know and be convinced of what the will of God is.

Once you know the will of God you can know that justice will be served for you. The only way you know the will of God is to study the Word of God.

Use your words. Enforce it. Don't be intimidated. Don't let the situation appear bigger than God.

I hate what the devil does to people. I hate sickness. I hate what people put up with. They need to be taught there is a new way of living that Jesus paid for.

My job, your job, the Church's job is to be sharers of good news. I believe we don't share because we're not convinced. My prayer is reading this book and studying the scriptures will convince you of what the Word of God says. There are too many stories and too many scriptures for you not to be—you're going to know too much to not be convinced.

Right now you might not be there. You might be intrigued, but that's about it. Just wait a little while. Let faith build in your spirit.

Help!
It's Dark Out Here!

As I shared earlier, when I got married, I was broke. God brought me my beautiful wife and I drug her through hell for the first few years of our marriage. I was supposed to be the head of my house, but we had no money. Everything we had was used and broken and dysfunctional. We owed a lot of people a lot of money. Everything that happened set off emotional fires. I made money. I just didn't make enough.

We loved God. We really truly loved God. I had an Old Testament degree. We led praise and worship at our church. But fear was my middle name. I was having panic attacks. I couldn't sleep at night. No one could figure out what was wrong with me. I had no peace. There's no peace when fear speaks.

Then, I got a tooth infection and I had to have a root canal done. My mouth was so sore that I could not sleep. I had taken two Tylenol every four hours for several days in a row. One night I was up because of the pain, and I was just reading the Tylenol box. I was alarmed to read that you cannot take Tylenol every four hours without stopping. If you do you will be taking more than they suggest. So thinking back on the last few days I realized that I had taken at least an extra dose each of those days, if not two extra doses. Fear started screaming, "OH MY GOSH, GARY! You've taken too many!"

Now, fear will also offer you a solution. That time, fear said, "Call Poison Control and find out." So, I called Poison Control and told them what I had been doing, that I had taken two tablets of Tylenol too many for the last three days. The first thing out of the girl's mouth was, "We have never had someone live that took that dosage." I screamed, "What do you mean? I just took two tablets too many each day for three days." She did not stop. "I already told you that we have never had someone live that took that dosage." Then she said, "Either you drive yourself to the hospital, or I'm sending an ambulance after you right now." I was shocked!

> *See, fear can warp your mind. And fear will make you pay. You think a hangnail could cause blood poisoning. That bump could be cancer. One credit mishap and you're going to go bankrupt. One rumor at work and you're going to lose your job.*

So I drove myself to the emergency room, and two guys were there pacing back and forth out front waiting for me! I walked in and my name was already on the dry erase board. It said, "Keesee—overdose." That's what it said.

Then, they ran a bunch of tests and the doctor walked in and said, "Why are you here? You don't have enough Tylenol in your system to cure a headache."

See, fear can warp your mind. And fear will make you pay. You think a hangnail could cause blood poisoning. That bump could be cancer. One credit mishap and you're going to go bankrupt. One rumor at work and you're going to lose your job.

Shortly after that, I got a call from an attorney filing a lawsuit over one of the many late credit accounts I had. I hit my breaking point. I gave up. I threw myself across my bed and I cried out to God. I had tried to do things myself. I had worked hard all day every day, but my life was chaos. My family was suffering. I couldn't do the things for them that I should have been able to do for them. My life felt like hell on earth.

So, I cried out to God and He said, "Philippians 4:19," which says, "But my God shall supply all your need according to his riches in glory by Christ Jesus" (KJV). Now, I knew that scripture, but I didn't KNOW that scripture. I didn't understand the Kingdom. God told me I had never learned how His Kingdom operates.

I told Drenda what the Lord told me, and we agreed to find out how the Kingdom operates. When I began to apply these laws, my life changed drastically. I got out of debt in two years!

I was a believer, but no one had taught me about the Kingdom of God or its laws—about living the Kingdom while you're here on the earth instead of waiting until you get to heaven. I had grown up in church. I was a Christian. But my life looked like everyone else's, except I had fire insurance—I was going to heaven. I was a good guy with a good heart, but I was clueless about life.

I knew all of the rules. I learned all of that stuff. And they didn't help me. No one had explained the Kingdom to me.

Living like that is like living in a dark room with no light.

Isaiah 60:2 tells us that a thick darkness is over the people of the earth, but the Lord rises upon us and His glory appears over us. Matthew 4:16 tells us that "the people living in darkness have seen a great light; on those living in the land of the shadow of death a light has dawned."

The light is Jesus, and the good news of the Gospel. Notice I didn't say the good news of attending church or the good news of doing good deeds or the good news of wearing proper clothing. For years the church has tried to get religion to sound like good news, but religious do's and don'ts aren't good news.

The good news is that people who were enslaved in sickness and poverty, death and disease are no longer enslaved. The good news is that you don't have to put up with fear. The good news is that you don't have to be enslaved by the rat race.

The good news of the Kingdom is that you can be free!

How Far Will You Let God Take You?

David was just a shepherd. He didn't have the title of leader. He demonstrated a solution to a problem. He took care of Goliath. He demonstrated the Kingdom of God. Then, he found himself hiding in a cave, surrounded by a bunch of guys who were disillusioned, in debt, frustrated and discouraged. But David showed them the Kingdom. He showed them that all things were possible. He went out without a sword and took down Goliath. And that encouraged them. They wanted to follow this man that had the faith and the courage to walk out the Kingdom. And they did. They became David's mighty men of valor.

In fact, their stories and exploits are recorded in the book of Chronicles. They completely changed their course. The Bible even tells us that they became wealthy. These broke, discouraged guys who were living in a cave gave today's equivalent of billions of dollars to help build the temple. They had learned from David. They had changed.

Mark 9:23 tells us that all things are possible to those that believe. We hear that and we celebrate, but we're not reading the fine print. It says all things are possible to those that believe. To those . Not to God, but to those who believe—that's you.

Just like those guys in the cave with David, how far God can take you depends on how much you'll let Him change you. In Ephesians 3:20, it says, "Now to him who is able to do immeasurably more than all we ask or imagine, according to his power that is at work within us." You don't have to wait on God. He wants a lot more done than you can even think of. He wants more impact. He's waiting for someone to rise to the challenge. He knows the world is waiting to hear your story. The world is waiting for someone who knows the truth about God. They're waiting for someone to tell them who they are in Christ. They want to know the potential future they have.

I was a shy kid. I would duck my head down in class. I hated standing up in front of people and having to say anything. When my parents would have parties, I would hide in my room. I would even hide out during parties that were thrown for me. One time, a teacher heard me talking to someone in the hallway and said, "Well, you do talk."

What kind of potential did I have then to do great things? None. Hiding in a room, or hiding in a cave, will get you nowhere. I needed to learn and change just like David's men needed to learn and change.

My life drastically changed when I met my wife, Drenda. I had a 1.3 Grade Point Average. She was a 4.0 student. She worked long hours. She was capable. She knew how to get things done. She was a possibility thinker. So, I married her, and God called us to sell insurance. That's a fantastic job for someone who is afraid to talk to people. Cold-calling people and talking about the lovely subject of dying—that's fun stuff. I died a thousand deaths every week when I sold insurance. I would lay in bed at night shaking. It wasn't comfortable. I didn't want to do it. I hated it. But I couldn't quit because I knew God had called me to it. He was teaching me. He was changing me.

See, God has too much invested in you to let you sit on the sidelines. He's going to make it uncomfortable for you. He's going to call you out into the deep water. He's going to give you vision and dreams and pull you out—sometimes KICK you out. It's not that He wants you to have that turmoil and discomfort; it's because He knows what you can do and how much you're going to love it when you get out there.

When God told us to start a church, I couldn't sleep for days. It was scary.

When he told us to host a marriage conference, I was scared spitless. I didn't know anything about marriage other than being married. So, I'd sit in my car and listen to these marriage tapes. We paid for this conference ourselves, and we had 250 people come to that little marriage conference. We did it afraid. I felt so vulnerable and insecure afterwards and I thought, "I am NEVER going to do that again."

A month or so later, my brother was waiting in the emergency room for someone to get stitches, and he started talking to a couple who was also waiting. When he told them his name, they asked him if he was related to me. They went on to tell him how they were nearly divorced, but that they had gone to our marriage conference and it had changed their lives.

See, there were things happening that we didn't know about. We had ventured out into that scary thing and amazing things happened. God was teaching me some things about stepping into the impossible.

In Matthew 25, we read the Parable of the Talents. The assignments were given to them based on what the master thought their ability was. The guy who was given the five talents was given an assignment that was bigger than he was. It was a ten-talent assignment. And, because he knew the master's heart, he embraced the harder assignment and went and ran with it. He knew the master was trying to help him. He knew he was trying to promote him. But that's not the typical response. Most people are like the one-talent guy. They shrink back. They're afraid. He buried his one talent. He had a wrong perception of his master, just like we have a wrong perception of God. But his master wasn't a hard taskmaster, and neither is God.

God is a rewarder. If we take care of His stuff, He takes care of our stuff. He's called you out to do impossible things, and with that comes reward.

I have countless examples of what happens when you change and become a possibility thinker—raising $2.5 million with only 300 people, building the Now Center, paying our builder the $1 million we owed him when the banking industry crashed, not knowing where the money would come from when God told us to start our television ministry—the list goes on.

I wish I could tell you it was so simple and so easy, but it wasn't. There were fearful things to face and impossible things to discuss. I'd like to say that I was so confident with God that it was no problem, that I'm the pastor and I'm so courageous —I'm just a person! All I can teach you is what I've walked through. In myself I have no confidence except for what He's taught me.

God has reinforced the same lesson in my life over and over and over again—He is a rewarder.

All things are possible to those that believe. God has bigger plans for you than you have for yourself. He wants you to embrace it. I guarantee you, if you will say "yes," He'll take you farther than you ever imagined.

How far will you let Him take you?

How Hungry Are You?

Once, when I was in Florida, I struck up a conversation with our taxi driver. He had come to the U.S. from Haiti prior to the earthquake. He told me how determined he and his cousin had been to get to the U.S.—they fasted and prayed for weeks. Then, when the opportunity came, they jumped on an overloaded boat, almost capsized multiple times and came to the U.S. Then he worked to be here legally.

Do you want to be free from anything in your life that badly?

How hungry are you for change in your life?

We have to stop crying out for survival to help us pay our bills and ask Him for opportunities.

Nearly every day, I get an email asking me to pray for supernatural debt cancellation for someone. I had one person ask me to pray in agreement with them that God would just cancel their debt.

I want to address this because, unfortunately, the Body of Christ has some mixed up ideas about this. Let me tell you once and for all:

Supernatural debt cancellation = PAY IT OFF!

See, asking for "supernatural" debt cancellation comes from a survivor mindset. You're a believer! Believers are supposed to look different. We're not supposed to be begging God to pay our bills. We're supposed to be looking for victory, not survival. We're supposed to show the world what the light looks like.

> *There are ideas around you all the time. You have the ability to make things different. Don't you want people to look at your life and say, "Wow! What happened to them? How'd they do that?" I want people to think your life is astonishing.*

You're the light of the world. You need to show people a different way of living. People should see your life as a sign pointing them in another direction. We have to change our mindset. God has already helped you. You have been made more than an overcomer.

He laid His life down to empower you and give you an amazing inheritance. You are supposed to have creative ideas. You have favor and the wisdom of God. You are the head and not the tail.

But people are always trying to stop—to find a place of rest, to get comfortable and escape the pressure. But there will always be people who need you. The Bible says the poor will always be with us. There will always be people who need answers. We can't run from the pressure. There is always going to be pressure to have more money. There will always be pressure.

I want to deal with your mindset. Because when I say "just pay it off," you probably can't see that. You can't really grab it. In Mark 6:37, Jesus told the disciples to feed the crowd when they had very little with which to feed them. Jesus said all things are possible to those that believe. They had no way to feed the masses and Jesus said, "Feed them." So, Jesus isn't coming to your pity party. You wouldn't want Him to. He would show up and say, "Take care of it. Deal with it. I have equipped you to win. God says YOU can do it."

You shouldn't be satisfied with mediocrity. You shouldn't see Friday as a goal. You shouldn't look forward to stopping. You're missing out on life! You might be comfortable sitting there with your payments made on time, but you're missing it. God wants to use you and you're missing it!

There are ideas around you all the time. You have the ability to make things different. Don't you want people to look at your life and say, "Wow! What happened to them? How'd they do that?" I want people to think your life is astonishing.

You can change your life, but you have to look for the opportunities. God has destined you to be different, but it depends on you.

How hungry are you?

Is Peace Really Possible?

People are always looking for peace.

There's the mom whose kids keep fighting, the businessman with the unstable career, the young woman on anti-depressants, the teenage boy on drugs, the couple that can't ever agree on their finances, the grandmother who can't sleep at night because she's worrying about her family—they're all hungry for peace.

The world is hungry for peace.

People spend money and time searching for peace. They buy things, hoping that those things will bring peace. But they're looking in the wrong places. They have it backwards.

Because peace is a product of the inside.

Peace isn't a feeling. The world thinks peace is a feel-good thing, but it isn't. Peace is a state of tranquility.

Jesus demonstrated true peace. In John 14:27, we see Jesus was letting the disciples know He was leaving. He said,

"Peace I leave with you, my peace I give unto you: not as the world giveth, give I unto you. Let not your heart be troubled, neither let it be afraid" (KJV).

Now, the disciples probably had a stomachache right at that moment. I can imagine what they were thinking.

"He can't leave! He calmed the storm when we were on the boat!"

"But He always knows how to calm our fears!"

"He helped us understand priorities and what life was about!"

"Every time we were afraid, He gave us courage!"

"He healed so many and raised them from the dead! We can't be confident without Him around!"

"Do you remember when He told us how to pay our taxes? What are we going to do?"

See, if you had one person to go to who had all of the answers for every situation you were in, who could calm your fears and who could calm the storms in your life with just one word, how do you think you'd act if he said he was leaving?

That's why Jesus said, "Let not your heart be troubled, neither let it be afraid." Because the disciples were troubled and afraid!

Jesus was their peace. They didn't know how to function without Him, or at least they thought they didn't. But Jesus was trying to tell them that it wasn't about Him. He was the Prince of Peace, but He had peace because of what He had on the inside—the Holy Spirit. And He was saying, "My peace (Holy Spirit) I give you."

See, the Holy Spirit is the one that counseled Jesus. Jesus walked by the power of the Holy Spirit. Acts 10 tells us that Jesus was anointed by God. He was one with the Father and could hear His voice. And He was passing that on.

Remember when the prodigal son was given the signet ring of his father? He was given the exact same authority. That's what Jesus was doing. In John 14:26, He says,

"But the Comforter, which is the Holy Ghost, whom the Father will send in my name, he shall teach you all things, and bring all things to your remembrance, whatsoever I have said unto you" (KJV).

Who gave Jesus all of those ideas while He was walking the earth? Who gave Him the answers? That's why God is the God of Peace—because He's the God of answers. He knows exactly how to handle every situation. The Bible calls Him a "Comforter." To comfort doesn't mean to pet, hug and love on. What comforts you when you're sick? HEALING! What comforts you when you need money? MONEY! What comforts you when you need an idea? IDEAS!

Now, I know life can be hard. It's easy to lose sight of peace. That's why the Bible tells us to fix our eyes on Jesus. The Holy Spirit will remind you of who you are, of your authority, that what the devil is trying to do shall not prosper, that your story isn't finished yet and that you're going to end up winning this game. When you believe Him and are comforted, joy will spring up in you.

See, the battle is over, my friend. You DO have someone to go to who has all of the answers for every situation you are in, who will calm your fears and who will calm the storms in your life with just one word; and He says He will never leave you or forsake you.

How can you not have peace if God Himself is with you? How can you walk around depressed?

It IS possible to have peace if God lives in you.

Take It Seriously

I want to talk about the whole man concept—how we're made up of spirit, soul and body, because many times Christians get so spiritually minded that they're no earthly good. Because we get busy chasing demons and the anointing, and running from meeting to meeting, but we forget to feed our kids. We get out of balance. We have to keep all three parts in balance to enjoy the goodness of God. Balance couldn't be more important.

I want to bring some things home. It's time to go there. So let's start with what the Word of God says. First Corinthians 6:19-20 tell us that our bodies are temples of the Holy Spirit and that we're to honor God with them. That means that our bodies carry the presence, the authority and the nature of God wherever we go.

See, God is limited to where we go—He can't go any farther than that. So if your body can't do the job it's supposed to do, God can't do what He wants to do. This is where we have to get a proper perspective. We have to know what and who we really are. We've read that we're temples, but what do we do with that? We might realize our bodies are important, but we don't think about them in terms of worship. We think worship is slow songs and goose bumps. But if you want to worship God, you honor Him and do what He says—with everything. So what does it look like to worship God with your body?

Well, Ephesians 5 tells us that we are to respect our physical bodies as Christ respected the Church. He made the Body of Christ holy. Your physical body is holy unto God. It is separated and consecrated. Imagine that you're looking at the most beautiful building you have ever seen—that's how God looks at you. He bought you with the blood of Jesus. There is no one like you on the earth. He made you radiant. Before you were born again, you were alive, but you weren't alive in Him. When you were born again, you became radiant. And then, holy and blameless. We are to keep our bodies holy and blameless. That is our act of worship to Him—keeping ourselves holy and blameless. It doesn't matter if you agree with that or not. That's what the Bible says.

So we see that we have a responsibility—to God—to handle our bodies properly. We see that our bodies are extremely important to God. So, I'm sure you can imagine why the devil hates the body so much. In fact, he wants to destroy your body. He wants to dishonor it. He wants you to misuse your body. He wants to make you filthy. He wants you to hate yourself and your features; to think your body is ugly or worthless; he wants you to devalue yourself. He wants you to defile your body. Because when you defile your body, you give Satan legal access to your life.

Norvel Hayes tells a story about two parents who called him because their son was in a trance. Something had happened to him. He was away at college, and he had fallen into this trance and no one could get him out. When Norvel arrived he found out that this young man had streaked across the campus naked, and at the end of the run he had basically became a zombie. Norvel began to pray for him. He prayed for eight hours. At the eighth hour green foam began to come out of that young man's mouth and he finally came out of the trance. See, that young man had defiled his temple and given Satan legal access to his life.

Now the culture will help you with this. They'll tell you that sexual sin is the norm. They'll try to get you to believe that mutilation is trendy. They'll tell you it's fun to run across campus naked. But you need to be aware. The culture degrades the body. No one should see you naked. We need to be modest. We're the temple of God. Only our spouses should see us without our clothes on. We need to teach our young people to dress modestly because the world definitely doesn't teach it.

Now, I know I'm stepping on toes here, but I'm going to take it one step further. I may get in trouble for this, but most of the time the tattooing and piercing stuff I see is degrading. Now, there are tasteful ways to decorate your body, but many times people get this stuff and wish they could change it later in life. You need to be wary of those things. Count the cost. Be careful. Your body is God's. Keep a proper perspective. Don't buy into the culture.

I'm not telling you any of this stuff to make you feel condemned. There is no condemnation here. We all fight this. That's why one of the fruit of the Spirit is self-control. The Spirit of God will help you—all you have to do is bring it to Him. Maybe you don't think you have the strength. Maybe you've been doing the same things for years and you don't know how to stop it. You have a chronic habit. Something is out of whack. Maybe the Holy Spirit has been dealing with you about it and you've been neglecting it. Ask God to help you. Above all else, His desire is to prosper you and for you to be in health.

I want to see you healthy, too. We're known for teaching you to prosper, but you can't do that if you're not healthy. Yes, God is a healer, but He made your body to heal itself, and you can avoid a lot of things if you'll take care of it the way you should.

I'm no exception. I know what it's like to be overweight. When I can't handle it I ask God to help me fix it. I need help to make a decision that sticks. I know that with God I can do anything, but I have to give my life and my body to Him. So do you.

So, remember that your body is a member of Christ Himself. Stop doing things with your body that give Satan access. Take it seriously that your body is a temple. Filter life through that and make the changes you need to make.

Here are few things that a panel of doctors in my church recommend:

- Stop using medicine to fix yourself. Fix your lifestyle and the medicine may not be needed anymore.

- Find balance in every area of your life.

- If you smoke, stop.

- Consider what you're eating and when you're eating it.

- Make changes to your diet. Use meat as a condiment rather than as a main course. Eat more fruits and vegetables.

- Get out there and get moving. Make exercise a way that you worship God.

- Try to cook at home as much as possible. Home cooked meals have less preservatives and bad ingredients.

- Eat regularly during the day. Your body is an engine that requires fuel. You need to fuel your body. Make sure that you're eating small meals during the day.

- Stop focusing on your weight and focus on your temple. When you are doing healthy things for your temple, you'll see the results.

- It's NEVER too late to make changes.

- You're in charge. No one has the authority over your body but you.

It's About the Journey in Between

A lady e-mailed me recently with a problem. Someone on Christian TV told her that, if she gave $72, she would receive a breakthrough in 72 hours. When she didn't have her breakthrough in 72 hours, she wasn't happy. So she e-mailed me.

See, some Christian TV programs tell you that you can give and everything will be taken care of. And, yes, giving is vital and sowing, and reaping is a key principle in the Kingdom of God, but we have to do a better job of how we explain it. Because giving itself, in itself, is just a formula.

Now, I've seen God do some amazing things in finances, but the risk for someone that doesn't understand how and why giving works is that they try to copy the formula, thinking that things will happen exactly the same way for them. But the power isn't in the formula. The formula is like the power lines. You can drive down the street and see power lines and know that all of the houses on that street are lit up because of those power lines, but the power lines are just the conduit. They carry the power, they are not the power. If those power lines aren't hooked up to the power source, then the houses won't be lit.

In the same way the formula of giving can work for you too—IF you're hooked up to the power source. Of course the power source is the Word which produces faith. When we are in faith, we can tap into the power source for our finances. But what does that look like? Most people think that money looks like money. Nope. Let me explain.

My friend raises hogs and, let me tell you, they smell. One day I asked him how he could stand living around that smell day in and day out. He looked at me and grinned and said, "Smells like money to me." You see, money is created in the marketplace, so it does not really look like money; it looks like something that is sold, which creates money. Most Christians are believing God for money when they should be believing God for the ideas to create money.

A lot of Christians are like a radio that isn't tuned into the right frequency. They may have the formula down but they are missing the instructions or reception completely because they are looking in the wrong direction. It even happened to the disciples.

Take a look at Mark 6:45-52. Jesus had just finished feeding 5,000 people with 5 loaves of bread and 2 fish. Then he sent His disciples ahead of Him in a boat and He went off to pray. Later that night they saw something on the water—it was Jesus.

And they were afraid! Here they had lived with the guy all this time! We can say we would have reacted differently, but we probably wouldn't have. It seems that most people posture themselves to receive from the familiar. You would've thought Jesus would be coming behind you in a boat, not walking on the water.

That's how we are with new ideas. If you're in construction, you believe for more construction jobs. If you're a waiter, you believe for more tips. You dismiss ideas that are outside of your comfort zone. You say, "It's bigger than me," or "I don't have any experience with that," and you set it aside. Thoughts are whirling past you, but you tell yourself, "It's not my field." You've trained yourself to look for the familiar, like Jesus coming in a boat.

But Jesus said three very important things that night from the water. He said, "Take courage. It is I. Don't be afraid."

- Take courage, because any new assignment will require you to handle greater responsibility, and you'll be tempted to be afraid of that. Or you just can't see how you would have time to tackle the learning curve to handle the new task so you dismiss it. However, if you're truly anticipating increase, you'll think different thoughts and embrace opportunity.

- "It is I." New ideas aren't always going to make sense to you. It's not important that they make sense to you. The voice of God can be easy to miss. He works with our passions and our makeup. He works with things we don't even know about ourselves. Those ideas are always going to be bigger than you are. You just need to pay attention and write it all down.

- Don't be afraid. Do something God thinks you can do, not something you think you can do. With God all things are possible, and He's going to strengthen you. If He gives you an idea, He must think you can do it with His help. You've got to train yourself to be open to new, unusual, weird ideas. Don't miss the direction and the timing.

Don't get discouraged. God is interested in the beginning and the end, but He's most interested in the journey in between. Take courage. It is really Him. Don't be afraid.

It's Already Finished

Hiroo Onodo was a Japanese soldier in WWII. He was highly skilled, having been trained to gather intelligence, and was a specialist in guerilla warfare. In 1944, he was sent to Lubang Island in the Philippines. Just months later, the island was conquered and the remaining Japanese soldiers headed into the jungle to hide.

But the soldiers had a problem. The war was over and they were still hiding. Despite several attempts to let them know the war had ended, they continued to hide. Several of the men finally came out, or passed away, but Onodo stayed in the jungle. He just couldn't believe that the war had ended.

Twenty-nine years later (yes, 29!) a student found him living in a cave. He still believed the war was going on. He had even killed and injured people mistakenly. When the student tried to get him to come home, he said his commanding officers were to come and retrieve him no matter what happened, and they hadn't done that. It took tracking down his retired leader to come and tell him the war had long been over. Twenty-nine years of Onodo's life had been wasted!

Terrible story, huh? Here's the saddest part: Onodo was living like a lot of Christians live—in survival mode—not knowing the battle is already finished.

In Luke 10:17-20, Jesus sent out 72 disciples and it says they returned with joy.

> **The seventy-two returned with joy and said, "Lord, even the demons submit to us in your name." He replied, "I saw Satan fall like lightning from heaven. I have given you authority to trample on snakes and scorpions and to overcome all the power of the enemy; nothing will harm you. However, do not rejoice that the spirits submit to you, but rejoice that your names are written in heaven.**

See, they realized that the demons were subject to them. They understood that the battle was finished.

The minute you understand that it is finished is the day you can live joyfully. It's not enough for your pastor to say you can have victory. It's not enough for you to hear, or read, that you can have victory. It's only when you experience the victory that your life will be changed. That's when you'll realize you're free, and that you have a future.

Jesus said He's given you authority. That's in red ink in my Bible. I don't care what your favorite Bible teacher says on the radio or what your circumstance is telling you, Jesus said nothing will harm you. Put the word "me" at the end and say it out loud, "Nothing will harm me."

Most people are looking outside of themselves for the answer, but YOU have been given the power to trample on the enemy's schemes. This is what the Bible is trying to tell us. What did David kill Goliath with? How many men did Gideon lead against the Midianites, only to stand by as they started killing each other because of confusion? How many pick axes did Israel need to break down the wall of Jericho? How many fertility specialists did Abraham and Sarah have to visit? How did Lazarus come out of the grave? Look at what God is showing us in His Word!

God woke me up one night with these words, "My people must change their mindsets. They're not thinking right. Their thoughts are holding them hostage. They're not thinking the thoughts of Christ. They're not thinking as victors think."

God wants you to know the war is over! There is victory!

In college, there was a guy who lived in the room next to me who had a severe lazy eye. He had no depth perception. Every night I would see him reading his Bible. One night, I walked by his room and he asked me to come in. He said, "I've discovered that Jesus paid for my healing!" He asked me to pray with him. We prayed and he received his healing. That was great, but he could have been set free from that earlier! He had just discovered the battle was over.

How many things have you lost or missed out on because you didn't know the battle was over?

So many people live under the lie that Satan is in charge, but you've been given authority to bind and to loose. You don't have to beg or cry. There doesn't need to be any hype. You just have to understand God's government. God is going to back up His Word. Then you can step into that government and enjoy the benefits of that Kingdom.

Any bondage in your life is simply a lack of truth. You've believed a lie.

The devil doesn't mind you knowing Matthew 28:18: "Then Jesus came to them and said, 'All authority in heaven and on earth has been given to me.'" That doesn't scare him a bit. He remembers when Jesus came out of the tomb. But Jesus isn't here.

Everyone knows God is powerful. That's not the key to your victory. No, what the enemy is scared spitless that you'll realize is Mark 11:22-24:

> **"Have faith in God," Jesus answered. "Truly I tell you, if anyone says to this mountain, 'Go, throw yourself into the sea,' and does not doubt in their heart but believes that what they say will happen, it will be done for them. Therefore I tell you, whatever you ask for in prayer, believe that you have received it, and it will be yours."**

Notice it says, "If you say to this mountain," but how do most people pray? They say, "Father, we come to you in the name of Jesus and ask you to _____." We've got it wrong. Religion has taught us to go to God.

Now, don't misunderstand what I'm saying. Jesus is teaching us how His government works. A mountain is something that stands in opposition to His government. Jesus didn't pray to God. He spoke to Lazarus. He spoke to the centurion. He spoke to the leper. He spoke to the wind and the waves. He didn't speak to God. He spoke to the demons. He spoke to the paralytic. Do you see what I'm showing you?

There isn't one time recorded where He asked God to do it. Jesus operated in delegated authority and heaven backed it up! He is our example!

These stories are written to show us how the Kingdom of God operates. So read the Word. Learn how the government operates. It will completely change your life! God's already done it all! What are you putting up with that you don't have to? What have you learned to live with? God doesn't play favorites! The battle is already finished.

Keep Gazing at the Truth

When Amy T. was 25 years old she started having headaches. Those headaches became more and more frequent. It got so bad that she would wake up every morning and go to bed every night with a migraine. The headaches forced her to withdraw from everything. She couldn't work. She didn't go outside. She was paralyzed by pain.

Amy was a newlywed, but she couldn't enjoy time with her husband. They would sit in the dark because any amount of light would trigger another migraine. If she had to drive at night she would have to wear sunglasses. If someone took her picture she would instantly get a migraine. So Amy did the thing you do—she went to see several specialists, and they sent her for tests. They looked for answers and came up with nothing. They told her they didn't know how to help her. They told her she should just try to manage her pain.

That was a death sentence to Amy.

So she went to the pain specialist and they put her on a program. They put shots into her skull. And we're not talking about 1, or 2, or even 5 shots—they put 23 shots in the back of her skull at her first appointment! At the second appointment it was 15 shots. She was getting shots in her forehead, the back of her head and her neck! And she wasn't even getting any better!

Okay. So you've been reading what I shared on healing. And now you're reading Amy's story and you're waiting to hear how she started believing God and then everything changed, right? Well, that's not what happened. See, Amy believed God the whole time. She knew the Word and that Jesus had paid for her healing, but it wasn't happening. So what was wrong? Did God just decide not to heal her? Have you been paying attention?

Healing is a PROMISE from God! If you're not convinced of that yet then you need to go back and read my earlier chapters. Read them—and your Bible—over and over again until you are convinced. Then decide that you're fed up!

That's exactly what happened to Amy. She got fed up. She decided that she didn't want to live the rest of her life "managing her pain." She knew better. She just had to do something about it. So she sought God. She got in the Word just like she had before, but this time something was different. This time when she read Romans 8:11 one particular word jumped out at her—quicken.

Romans 8:11 says:

> **But if the Spirit of him that raised up Jesus from the dead dwell in you, he that raised up Christ from the dead shall also quicken your mortal bodies by his Spirit that dwelleth in you. (KJV)**

Then the Holy Spirit revealed that the word "quicken" translates into "restore." When Amy looked up "restore" in the dictionary it said "to take back to its original state."

And that's the word Amy stood on—every single day. She had

to battle and fight, but she kept her focus on that word and she got her healing.

So what happened? What changed? Let's look at an important story from the Bible to get some understanding.

In Numbers 21 we read the story of the bronze snake on the pole. Here the Israelites had gotten frustrated with God. They had complained and spoken against God, so God had sent fiery serpents into the camp and they bit the Israelites, and many of them died. At that point the people realized they had sinned and they asked Moses to pray for them. When Moses prayed, God gave Moses a way of escape for the people—the bronze serpent on the pole.

So we see the Israelites had a problem. They had a serious attitude problem. They lost sight of God. They were impatient. They lost sight of the goodness of God. So God didn't just take the snakes away. He had a better plan. He wanted to deal with their heart problem. He had Moses put the snake on the pole to remind them of their problem. In order to correct the problem they had to turn and look at it. They had to meditate on the promise of healing from God. They had to make heart changes in order to receive.

Jesus was the pole for us. Jesus was the solution to our problems. He was our way of escape. But Jesus isn't here. We can't physically turn and gaze on Jesus like the Israelites did with the pole, so He gave us something in His place—the communion table.

Taking communion is not a religious event. When we come to the table we're to remember what Jesus paid for—what He gave us, what He gave for us. I see that cup at the communion table and I'm reminded of the blood covenant, and I know that He has taken my sin and that I now have access to all the promises—to everything God says is mine.

When you eat the bread and drink the cup you proclaim the Lord's death. You are proclaiming to yourself—for YOURSELF—that communion represents the covenant—the promises. Just like the Israelites had to come and gaze at the pole, judge themselves and stop and evaluate their relationship to God, we need to do the same. Communion is our opportunity to do that.

So what does this have to do with Amy's story? After all, she wasn't complaining or speaking against God. She knew what God had promised. She didn't have a heart problem. But was she looking at the pole? Was she gazing on the covenant? When she turned, gazed, stopped and judged, the Holy Spirit starting correcting her. He started correcting her mouth. She stopped saying things like, "my migraines." She realized and corrected the little ways she had been focusing on the problem.

Do this. Gather your family in a time of need to take communion—you don't have to do it at church. Come to the table and remember what Jesus paid for. Then judge yourself. Recognize you need God and remind yourself every day if you need to. Meditate on the promise of healing from God and make heart changes in order to receive it.

Keep gazing on the truth from God's Word.

Keep Shooting

I received a big box from Montana. In it was an antelope head. Yes, I said antelope head.

The previous year at that time, a group of guys up there asked me to come teach and hunt. They had gotten ahold of my book *Faith Hunt*, and they wanted to learn the principles and see them in action. So, I went up there to teach and then the next day we went hunting for antelope.

We went out for about 30 minutes, climbed over this ridge, and saw this herd of antelope. Now, keep in mind that antelope are the second fastest animals in the world. They're second only to the Cheetah. Drenda and I had come into agreement for the antelope and, sure enough, there he was standing broadside about 275 yards from me. I will have to admit I am not the greatest rifle shot. As Ohio does not allow rifles to be used for deer, I do not get to take shots at 275 yards very often. So I shot and missed. At the shot, the antelope all starting running, all except one, the buck that I was shooting at. Sadly, I shot 3 more times at that buck and did not touch him. My gun was now empty. I yelled to Tim to give me his gun, and I took one more shot and I dropped the buck.

Now, what I did not tell you is that all the guys that had taken me out to hunt were waiting to see how *Faith Hunt* really works in the natural. When the buck had stayed in place while the rest had run off they all went nuts. They all started dialing people up on their phones saying, "It was just like the book! They all ran away but that one! The buck was held by spiritual law!"

Oh, it was a great story because I had the victory. But the truth was I had missed the antelope the first 4 times I shot. My story was really one of failure but I kept shooting.

What happened? Why do we miss sometimes? Why do we deal with failure and disappointment?

Okay, in Luke 4 the Spirit of God—not Satan—led Jesus to be tempted. Why would God do that? Because Satan is the god of this world. He has legality here in the earth. He has a legal right to contest what God is doing here. So, to make it legal for Jesus to walk the earth, **Satan had to have the opportunity to present to Jesus what he had presented to Adam.** Jesus had to be tempted in order to maintain the authority that God had placed in Him. Jesus resisted with the Word of God every single time. He stayed in agreement with heaven. Satan couldn't bring Him out of agreement.

He can't stop what God is doing, but he can test our agreement. If he can bring us out of agreement, then we stand subject to him. He isn't going to give up territory just because.

When you launch out on a God-idea, you will probably deal with some issues. That catches young believers off guard. We need to teach people that they will have to pass some tests. They will have to deal with Satan. Unlike God, who knows your heart, the only way the enemy can find out where you really stand is by putting the pressure on. If out of your mouth comes the Word and the anointing, he'll say, "WHOA" and he'll back off. But if you agree with him, he won't be concerned with you. He really doesn't care if you're going to heaven as much as he wants to prevent you from bringing heaven to earth.

The Bible says that the God of peace will soon crush Satan under your feet. It says the grace and the empowerment of God are with you—you've been empowered to win. You've been given the grace to deal with Satan when he messes with you. As you exercise that grace, God is going to crush him under your feet.

So, persevere! Persevere with the Word, by the Spirit. Constantly remind yourself of what God has said about you. And remember that you've already won, even when you miss. So keep shooting.

Keeping Unity in Your Marriage

If you've ever fallen into a pattern of bickering with your spouse, you know how easy it is to stay there. And that's just what the enemy wants. Because he knows that if he can keep you fighting over the dirty laundry, who's on bath duty, money or anything else, then he can keep you out of unity and away from your inheritance in the Kingdom of God. His greatest goal is to divide and conquer, and too often we let him.

Ephesians 6:12 reminds us that our enemy is not flesh and blood, but the rulers of the darkness of this world. Why do we forget that? Why are we willing to practically wage war with the person we're supposed to love most over the most insignificant things? Are the petty things like him not emptying the trash or her buying that extra pair of earrings really worth you missing out on the promises of God? No!

So how do we stop looking at our mate as our enemy, and how do we restore unity to our marriages?

1. Make sure there is no sin in your life. Sin not only destroys unity between you and your mate, it destroys unity between you and God.

2. Don't compare yourself or your spouse to others. No couple is perfect. Don't be deceived. Remember, you only see people's public face, not their private struggles.

3. Focus on the positive in your spouse. Think on the good points instead of the faults. We all have faults. Human nature is to hide our own faults and point out the weaknesses in others. God sees you both as valuable. Look at your spouse the same way.

4. Pay attention to what you're saying. Use your words to build up, not tear down. Realize how much power your words have.

5. Pray together. If you've never prayed together, or if it's been awhile, it will be awkward and uncomfortable. Do it anyway.

6. Learn more about the differences between you and your spouse as a man and a woman. We communicate differently! The more you understand that, the less communication breakdowns will occur in your marriage.

7. Really think about whether you're placing your needs over those of your mate. Selfishness can easily squash any hopes of unity.

8. Forgive. Holding onto an offense or hurt does nothing to help you. It only turns into bitterness.

9. Say you're sorry! Being too prideful to admit when you're wrong only builds walls of separation in your relationship.

10. Be friends! This is another one that might be awkward, especially if you've been bickering. But make plans anyway. Go do something fun together.

11. Set goals together and accomplish them as a team. Many of us show ourselves are valuable team members at work, in class and in sports, but we'd be embarrassed if those same people saw how we work (or don't work) together with our spouses. Change!

12. Have sex! The marriage bed is the healing oil that makes the two one flesh.

Most importantly, commit, or recommit, your marriage to God. He can help you recognize when your marriage is under attack, free you from any insecurities or failures that are preventing you from being one in your relationship and give you an understanding of His design for marriage.

Love— the Ultimate Reality

1 John 4:16

> **And so we know and rely on the love God has for us. God is love. Whoever lives in love lives in God, and God in him**.

God loves YOU!

Press the pause button on your life and think about what that means to you personally, at this very moment. It's pretty incredible to think that the Almighty God—the One who made heaven and earth—loves you, cares about you and is interested in you.

God's love is a simple, beautiful, eternal fact. The truth is, no matter what you've done or failed to do, what your past holds or your present looks like, God's love for you doesn't change. It can't. God IS love. His essence—His very existence— is love. It's simply impossible for God to stop loving you.

With God's love comes hope and confidence. As we allow God's love to serve as the anchor of our lives, it provides safety when the storms of life rage against us. Because of His love, we have hope

. . . we can trust . . . there is rest . . . we enjoy freedom . . . we are confident that in all things God works for our good. Stand firm in the knowledge that nothing can separate you from God's love!

Perfect love casts out fear because of the truth that the person who loves you will do anything for you. Lay down their life for you. That's exactly what Jesus did. Not only did He take our sin and punishment, He defeated death itself and rose again so that we could live free from darkness. He punched the enemy's lights out and put him under our feet.

> ───✍───
> ## Perfect love casts out fear because of the truth that the person who loves you will do anything for you.
> ───✍───

If God is for you ("for you" meaning on your team, backing you up, holding you in His arms, protecting you) then WHO can be against you? (Romans 8:31.)

Let the love of Father God and all He has done for you saturate your life. Let it become your greatest reality, your most treasured thought, your greatest security.

Loyalty– the Pathway to Promotion

Are you loyal?

Wait. Before you answer, consider this: How well do you follow instructions from someone in authority? When your leader gives you something to do that you don't really want to do, how do you act? Do you take the assignment and run with it? Or do you get offended and start complaining to the people around you?

Now that you've answered those questions, I'll ask you again: Are you loyal?

As I explained earlier, the authorities in our lives are established by God to help us, protect us, mold us and mentor us. And some of us soak that up because we've learned—probably the hard way—that submission to the leadership or authorities God has placed in our lives gives us an advantage. But some people don't think they need to submit to or be loyal to anyone, or they think that they only need to be submissive and loyal to certain people or in specific situations. And that is where things get dangerous.

The Bible tells us that those who have been given a trust must prove loyal, and we've all been given a trust—or responsibilities—of some sort. We are required to be loyal to the person that gave us the trust or the responsibilities. So many people want promoted in business and in ministry, but they aren't loyal to the leaders in their lives. Loyalty is the pathway to promotion.

So how do we know if we're really loyal? What does loyalty look like or, even more importantly, what does disloyalty look like?

One of the first ways to recognize disloyalty is to look for an independent spirit. While loyal people follow instructions, seek to please leadership and desire to be problem solvers, the independent spirits want to do things their way. They think their ideas are better than those of leadership. They begin to do things a little bit differently than the way they were asked to do them. They bend the rules, even if only subtly. And if and when leadership calls them on it, they quickly move to the next phase of disloyalty—offense.

You will be offended and you will offend at some point in your life. Loyal people forgive and move on. Disloyal people don't. They take it personally. Then, because they're carrying that offense, they become passive—the third phase of disloyalty. They stop showing up. They withdraw. Think about it. When you feel offended by someone are you generous toward that person—with your giving, your time, your attention, in serving them? Nope. Offended people stop doing.

And because offended, passive people are too busy watching instead of doing, they become critical—the fourth phase of disloyalty. They talk about the problems and never offer solutions. They blame leadership and never take responsibility. Conversely, loyal people realize that there will always be problems and that they play a role in fixing them. Loyal people know that we do it together.

The only thing disloyal people do together is get political—the fifth phase of disloyalty. This is when they get a little gutsy. They no longer just criticize leadership in front of those closest to them, but they start to draw others in to build a case against leadership and to have a forum for their complaints. They need justification. And when they've got their group of supporters, they move into phase six of disloyalty—deceit.

Disloyal people are almost always deceived. They think of themselves more highly than they should. They forget their teachers and how they got where they are. They forget to be grateful for those that have laid the path before them. Deception tells them, "You're big," and "They don't appreciate you." And so disloyal people get bold and openly rebel—phase seven of disloyalty. They put it all out there. They blog about it. They tell everyone they talk to about the offense.

Then they start attracting others like them—rebels who are also offended easily. And so they come to a crossroads—begin the whole process over again or change and submit. Either way, if a disloyal person has come to this eighth phase, an "execution" of some sort has to take place.

So, are you in one of these phases? Is it said about you that you're loyal? Do your employers, your spouse, your friends and your pastor call you loyal? If your answer is yes, that's great. If you know that you've been in one of these phases, though, it's not too late to change. Your emotions have nothing to do with it. You make the choice to be loyal. You don't have to feel loyal to be loyal.

Once you get this most important lesson in your life you will know how to respond to assignments, carry some weight and be trusted with the bigger-than-life things God has for you. One important truth you also need to remember: God backs up the loyal.

Pass the Test

God made you promises. He gave you a word in your life. He told you something amazing that He wants to help you do. He may have even given you a glimpse of what your life will be like when those things come to pass. Then you began waiting.

And you have a hard time waiting. You want those promises right now! Waiting for that word to come to pass is taking too long. In fact, it's taking so long that you're starting to wonder where God is.

So what do you do? Do you go after it on your own? Do you try to shortcut God and do it in your own timing, with your own strength and by your own power? Or do you keep waiting because you recognize your situation for what it really is—a TEST?

The dictionary defines a test as a procedure intended to establish the quality, performance or reliability of something, especially before it is taken into widespread use.

God uses tests in the same way—to establish us, to complete us, to promote us and, especially, to build our character.

You see, God's desire is to work His character in us. And just as Jesus was led into the wilderness, God allows us to be led into tests to build our character and to determine whether or not we can handle the assignments that He wants to give us. Only we can control how quickly we pass each test by making the right choices and the right decisions during them.

But we often see tests as something negative. We spend so much time looking at the test that we forget about the reward we will receive for passing. Then we get weak, we quit, we let go of the promises and we let go of what God said.

Then, like the stubborn and unbelieving Israelites stuck in the wilderness, we have to take the same test again and again and again.

So what do we need to do to pass the test the first time?

Pray. Know the Word. Listen to the Holy Spirit. Guard and examine your heart. Examine your motivations. Be a person of integrity. Submit yourself to the leaders that God has placed in your life. Be teachable. Be coachable. Be willing to serve. Be willing to wait patiently. Don't try to shortcut God.

And while you're waiting, hold onto that word God has given you. Remind yourself of it in the midst of the tests and trials. Remember that God loves you and that He wants to equip you with everything you need to pass the test. Ultimately, remember that the test is part of your training for a place of promotion for which God is training you. Passing the test is worth it!

Possibility Thinking

Most mornings, I grab my cup of coffee and scan the headlines of *The Wall Street Journal* to stay on top of the recent financial news. However, lately there's been so much doom and gloom that I have to watch out. When the world is washed in fear, it's easy to get caught up in the "earth- curse system" way of thinking.

We can renew our minds to God's unlimited Kingdom, but the curse of lack, poverty and fear is around us everyday, everywhere we look. For instance, most people continue to rely on debt as their way of life. But it doesn't have to be that way. I found that most people can be debt free, but they don't believe it.

For me, for you, for the millions of hard-working mothers and fathers just trying to "get by," the first step toward getting out of debt is to re-educate ourselves about ALL the financial possibilities that exist. The fact is we have all been brainwashed to believe that the debt system is the system of choice. No one really believes that they can be free. Instead, everyone focuses on payment amounts, not cash.

For Drenda and me, this re-education began as soon as we came to the agreement that we were finished with living in debt.

We decided that we were going to trust God to teach us His system. Not surprisingly, the Lord was standing by ready and willing.

My mind began to have thoughts I'd never thought before. In the night, when I was lying in my bed, the Holy Spirit would bring ideas and concepts to me that I had never thought possible. I couldn't shake these ideas. Eventually, I started playing with and meditating on these new concepts. I was a financial consultant, and I was shocked one day, playing with my financial calculator, to find out that a family I was currently working with could be out of debt in less than seven years, including their home mortgage, on their current income. At first, I thought I must have made a mistake. I went through my numbers again and again. I recalculated the same plan over and over, and to my amazement, I found out that my calculations were correct.

> *The point is, despite the fact that the situation may look bad and the economy is in trouble, there are always answers. We just need to be possibility thinkers rather than problem focusers.*

The family I had been meeting with was in trouble financially. They were living month to month as most Americans in debt do. But amazingly, these financial concepts the Holy Spirit was showing me could help not just me or this particular family, but ANYONE else pay off their mortgage and their credit cards in just a few years. This particular family was shocked to know that debt-free living was possible.

The point is, despite the fact that the situation may look bad and the economy is in trouble, there are always answers. We just need to be possibility thinkers rather than problem focusers. You may need just a little knowledge to turn your life around. We have to remind ourselves that our hope doesn't line up with the credit trap or in the economy or even in our current job. Things around us can and will change, but one thing will never change. We are part of a limitless Kingdom! So here is the test, what do you think about all the time? Do you think about the negatives? Or do you think about the ideas and visions that bubble up out of your spirit? If you will take the time to retrain how you think about life, life will change for you. The Kingdom of God will do just what the Bible says it will do; you can depend on it.

Your Story

Hebrews 11:8

By faith Abraham, when called to go to a place he would later receive as his inheritance, obeyed and went, even though he did not know where he was going.

This mission on earth is going to take more courage than faith, because it takes courage to act on your faith, to step out of the boat and to walk on God's Word. It takes courage to leave the familiar. One of my favorite chapters in the Bible is Hebrews 11 because it's the "Faith Hall of Fame." It lists all the people in the Bible who acted in faith and changed their world as a result. When you study this chapter, you recognize that there are certain traits that all people of faith exhibit.

1. People of faith view things differently than people who are surviving. Survivalists run and take cover. They don't engage.

2. People of faith look for the open doors. They're constantly expecting God to fling open a door any second, so they are always conscious of their surroundings.

3. People of faith are characterized by optimism because they serve a God who never has a bad day.

4. People of faith put themselves in a place to hear revelation from God in their spirits and to act on that revelation in this natural realm. They hear from heaven and act it out on earth.

5. People of faith leave behind familiar ground for unknown territory. If you want to do the impossible, you have to let go of the possible. We can't camp out in yesterday's victory. God is always on the move!

6. People of faith act in courage, even though they may feel afraid. I've learned that you've got to be aggressive in this life. You've got to be on the ball. You've got to be looking, seeking and on a mission to respond to God's direction every day.

7. People of faith cause lost people around them to ask questions because they receive God's voice. By revelation, you should be an island in the midst of a dark place, where people can say, "There is something about that person. I've got to have that. I'm going to go find out what it is."

8. People of faith have BIG vision because they believe in a BIG God. I always say that your vision needs to be bigger than you. Why would God give you a life vision that you could complete in your own resources and strength? He's going to give you a God-sized vision!

9. People of faith see possibility and work hard to make it a reality. They seize every opportunity. I'm amazed at the way some people just won't MOVE.

This usually means they have a poverty mindset. God could be waving a flag and saying, "Hey! Over here's a gold mine!" But people with a poverty mindset think, "That's too much work. Surely that can't be God." They don't even get the picture of possibility.

I have no doubt that right now, our stories of faith are being written. I also know that many, many people reading this book will be a part of the Faith Hall of Fame, joining those who have gone before us! We are people of faith, and we have the same anointing that Jesus had to change our world. Just like Abraham, we're leaving behind the places we've camped out, and we're heading toward the bright future God has for us. When we get to heaven, we'll remember this time, this season in our lives, when we made a solid commitment to lay aside the ordinary, the mundane, the average and be the heroes we were made to be. We do not need to waste time watching hero movies, we're writing our own story—we were born to be someone's hero!

The Favor Factor

I think favoritism gets a bad rap. We claim favoritism isn't fair when it's directed toward someone else, but we sure don't mind if it's coming our way.

I didn't mind when, years ago, my friend who worked at a car dealership called me to let me know that he could get me a really great deal on a new car because it had hail damage.

My kids didn't complain when I bought each one of them a car when they turned 18 just because they're my kids.

And you probably wouldn't complain if your cashier gave you an extra 20 percent off your transaction the next time you were at the store, right?

See, favor means "standing in a place of advantage." Sometimes you need just a little favor to push you over something in life. Favor will put you in front of great men and women you may never have had a chance to be in front of.

But people can't do it all.

Last year my family went to Long Island, New York for a vacation. I was out in the water and on the beach just enjoying the sun and water. Since the sun was so bright, I wore my expensive sunglasses out into the water. I wasn't going far out. In fact, I was only in waist-high water so I thought nothing about wearing my sunglasses. But out of nowhere came a huge wave that washed entirely over me, and my sunglasses were gone.

Now, those sunglasses were my favorite pair and I didn't want to lose them. I immediately cried out, "No! In the name of Jesus, I will not lose those glasses! Holy Spirit, show me where they are!" I then asked my two daughters who were on the trip with me to help me find them. We walked all around and felt the bottom with our feet. This went on for about 20 minutes, and we couldn't find them. I went back up to the shore and sat down with my wife, Drenda, telling her what had happened and that I was not going to lose those glasses. My plan was to go back out and look for them again, but Drenda suggested that we go for a walk first and then she would help me.

We walked down the beach about three-fourth's of a mile. Just as we were about to turn around and head back, a wave rolled in and I was shocked to see my sunglasses on top of that wave! My glasses came sliding in with that wave and skidded to a stop at my feet! Drenda and I just looked at each other in shock and awe!

Favor will change your life.

"But, that's just you, Gary. God favors you because you're a pastor."

Here's the thing you have to understand—there's a whole bunch of room in God's house. Anyone can have favoritism with God. John 1:12 says, "Yet to all who did receive him, to those who believed in his name, he gave the right to become children of God."

And John 15:15 says,

> **I no longer call you servants, because a servant does not know his master's business. Instead, I have called you friends, for everything that I learned from my Father I have made known to you.**

You're not a servant to God. You're His child and His friend. A servant doesn't know the master's business, but children and friends do. We're not servants in God's house. We're part of the family. We can ask questions about the family business. We can know what God is doing. We have the FAVOR, and we have a huge advantage.

Several years ago I had preached all day and was catching a red eye flight back from California to Ohio. I had 3 weekend services to preach when I got home and I was already tired. As I was heading to the airport I was talking to Drenda on the phone and she said, "Let's agree that you can fly home first class." I said "Okay," so we prayed. Now, I almost never fly first class, but sometimes if I really want to rest I will upgrade my seat. When I got to the airport, there were no first class seats available to upgrade to. In fact there was a waiting list of about 15 people who wanted to upgrade. So no chance.

As I got on the plane and sat down, I noticed a small commotion in front of me. A man wanted to sit next to his wife, but no one would switch seats with him or her. No one wanted the middle seat for this 4-hour red eye flight. Finally, I told her that I would give up my aisle seat and take a middle seat so that they could sit together. The stewardess seemed very pleased that someone would make a way for this to happen. So I ended up sitting back in about row 27 in the middle.

About 30 minutes into the flight they started to serve the economy seats their normal drink and peanuts. The first class curtain had been drawn, but you could smell a full meal being served to the first class guests. All of a sudden here comes that same stewardess down the aisle with a full first class tray in her hands. She walked all the way back to me and said, "I thought you might be hungry." Well, that was great, because I *was* hungry. But that wasn't all. She made trip after trip to bring me refreshments. About an hour after the meal, she brought me a full snack tray. Remember this was only happening to me, not anyone else in all of the economy seat area of the plane. An hour later she brought me a hot chocolate chip cookie and a drink. That was all the people around me could take. The lady next to me retorted, "All right, *who are you?*"

God is like those parents who have stickers of their kid's accomplishments on the bumpers of their cars. He is proud of you, and He loves showering you with things that excite you.

I enjoyed the favor of God on that flight because I am a child of God. I was tired, doing Dad's business and He was saying, "Hey, you take care of my business, I'll take care of you."

We all can live first class in an economy world if we just will know who we are and Whose we are. Favor in life comes from knowing God!

John 14:26 tells us that the Holy Spirit will teach us all things. Talk about favor! God Himself is on your side! You have access to inside information! God will help you live life before the devil even knows you're there. You can have wisdom in every situation.

Having favor may not be "fair" in terms of how the world looks at things. I'm fine with that, because I know that God wants to show us off. He wants others to see His favor in our lives. He wants to draw people to you who may not even know why they like you! But they all like chocolate chip cookies, and the smell will bring them over for a look. They'll ask, "Who *are* you?"

God is like those parents who have stickers of their kid's accomplishments on the bumpers of their cars. He is proud of you, and He loves showering you with things that excite you.

So, favoritism has gotten a bad rap. Who wouldn't want the favor of God? It's available to anyone.

I like favor, and I'll take all the favor I can get.

How about you?

The Generosity Factor

1 John 5:14

> **This is the confidence we have in approaching God: that if we ask anything according to his will, he hears us. And if we know that he hears us—whatever we ask—we know that we have what we asked of him.**

As we launch out into our future, we must make sure of one very important thing: we must know the will of God. Without it there can be no faith or victory. Our confidence in knowing God's will allows us to fight the fight of faith, knowing we have the victory every time! Conversely, not knowing the will of God allows the enemy to easily deceive us and cause us to back down. So, before we can ask God to help us prosper in life, we must be convinced that it is the *will of God* that we prosper. THEN we can KNOW that we will prosper.

So what does God really think about money? For many years churches have taught that money was evil and that people who really love God would not allow themselves to get involved with money. But the truth of the Word teaches us that money is very important to God and that He wants you to have it. Second Corinthians 9:8-11 tells us that it is God's will that you have the ability to be generous on EVERY occasion. Think about that—Paul says God wants you to be rich enough to be generous on *every* occasion. You must have more than enough money to be able to do that in peace. You see, God is generous and His Word says that He rains on the just and the unjust. Paul says that Christians who have money and are helping people with their money will cause those same people to praise God, because they see that you cared for them in the name of the Lord. (2 Corinthians 9:13.)

We don't worship money, but money *is* a very important aspect of life. As long as there are people in the earth who have needs and problems, we—as Christians, who represent God—can never have too much money. Money in the earth realm provides answers and solutions to life's problems. The problem with money is not really a problem with the money itself, but rather with the heart of those who *trust in* money and not in God. People who worship money and pursue money only for themselves can hurt other people through greed, destroying their lives through illegal profits and wrong priorities.

Money is simply a tool. It will magnify what our hearts worship. If a person has a good heart, then money will be an extension of that good heart. Money allows you to increase your influence of good to those around you. This is what Paul was referring to when he described how money affects a righteous man: "He (the man who has prospered) has scattered abroad his gifts to the poor; his righteousness endures forever" (2 Corinthians 9:9, parenthetical mine).

Paul is saying that this person has great influence. He's saying that what that generous person does with his or her money is righteous and will be remembered forever by those helped and by God.

Start where you are and be generous to someone before the day ends.

The Honor Code

Matthew 13:54-58

> Coming to his hometown, he began teaching the people in their synagogue, and they were amazed. "Where did this man get this wisdom and these miraculous powers?" they asked. "Isn't this the carpenter's son? Isn't his mother's name Mary, and aren't his brothers James, Joseph, Simon and Judas? Aren't all his sisters with us? Where then did this man get all these things?" And they took offense at him. But Jesus said to them, "Only in his hometown and in his own house is a prophet without honor." And he did not do many miracles there because of their lack of faith.

Most of us are familiar with this scripture that tells us Jesus couldn't do many works in His hometown. You might even remember that the Bible says it was because of their "lack of faith." But the problem wasn't that the people in Jesus' hometown didn't believe God, it was that they didn't honor Jesus.

You see, Jesus was too familiar. They knew His family. They thought they knew as much as He did. They didn't value anything

He was saying or doing. They told Him to prove Himself. They didn't honor Him. And we'll never be able to receive from someone that we don't honor.

Take the example of Elijah. During the time of famine, God sent Elijah to a widow in Zarephath for help. Why Zarephath? Wasn't there a widow in Israel that could've fed Elijah? Apparently there was no widow in Israel that honored Elijah enough for God to be able to use her. But the widow in Zarephath did honor God and Elijah and, in turn, she received.

Peter is another example. The guy had fished all night. You know he was tired. He was done for the day. They were cleaning their nets when Jesus told him to go back out. Peter honored Jesus. He obeyed and he received. Can you imagine how different the story might have been if Peter had acted like we do today? Imagine Peter saying, "I'm sorry, Jesus. I'm really worn out. This will have to wait until tomorrow. I'm going to get some rest."

Are you shaking your head? You should be. This is what is happening in our country and in the church. We have thrown aside the culture of honor. The Bible says that "the wicked freely strut about unopposed when what is vile is honored among men." This is what is happening right now. The enemy has always tried to devalue and dishonor authorities. He uses gossip and offenses to gain influence in our culture. He has a heyday when people lose sight of what is true and what is honorable.

So we have to fight to reestablish a culture of honor—a place where integrity means something. Clearly, just knowing that God has placed authorities in our lives to help us isn't enough. We have more to do. But what? Well, when we read further, we see that not only does God require that we subject ourselves to authorities, but that He directs us to "render respect to whom respect is due, and honor to whom honor is due" (Romans 13:7 AMP).

So how do we do that? The first thing we need to do is understand the difference between respect and honor. Don't mix them up. Respect is earned. Honor is given. We respect people for what they do. Honor, however, is a necessity—a requirement we give to the office, to the position. You may not respect a person, their beliefs, their ideas or their expectations, but if they have authority, they deserve honor.

When you honor something you treat it as if it's valuable. You esteem it. You look at it. You set it someplace safe. You lift it up above other things. It's important to you. Honoring a person is no different. When you honor a person you serve them. You value them. You tend to the relationship. You encourage them. You elevate them. You esteem them as better than yourself.

So the Honor Code is about more than leaving the right amount of money for the candy you took in the unattended box at the office. It's about more than being trustworthy and honest. The Honor Code is about choosing to live your life to please God. It's about realizing that you can't receive from the people you aren't willing to honor and that God might just be trying to use those very same people to get something amazing to you.

We have so much stuff and things that take our time that we don't honestly know what to honor. Thank God He tells us because in the end we're going to stand before Him thinking we've done this great work, and He's going to ask: "How did you honor your kids? Did you spend time with them? Did you honor your marriage bed? Or did you look at pornography and watch movies where the people committed adultery? Did you honor your body? Did you honor others as better than yourself? Or did you gossip and devalue others? Did you honor your father and mother?"

When it's all said and done, will you be able to answer "yes" when God asks you, "Did you render honor to whom honor was due?"

The Honor of Defending Freedom

Recently, after returning home from a conference, I witnessed evidence of the true condition of our country. I was at the airport and there stood a woman and her young son. In her hand she held a sign welcoming her husband home from his service in Iraq. She and her son stood alone.

This man that I didn't know had, by choice, laid his life on the line to protect me, to protect my family, my country and my freedoms, yet no one was there, at the airport, to give him the honor he deserved.

What has happened to our nation? We give honor and respect to musicians, actors, politicians and athletes and neglect honoring and respecting those that truly deserve it. We're so busy worrying about getting along with an opinionated coworker, not upsetting an out-of-line family member and having ourselves be "liked" that we don't even realize we're FAILING God's test!

The church has helped by preaching tolerance, acceptance and social justice. We've embraced sin while embracing the sinners. We've become complacent and been lulled to sleep by the world. They've told us not to judge them and we've listened. And all the while, those that don't want righteousness are continuing to take our freedoms until we will have none.

If there was an army attacking New York City right now we would all be mobilizing ourselves, preparing to fight a battle, but what many don't realize is that an army IS attacking our country right now. It's not a physical army but one that is steadily and deceptively using our Internet, our radios, our televisions and carefully placed people to strip us of our freedoms little by little every day.

Oh, and the enemy has done a great job of keeping you silent. He wants you to be easy to get along with. He loves that you're afraid to rock the boat—afraid of confrontations. But the Bible says we are never going to get along with the unrighteous—they will always despise us. In fact, Jesus said He came not to bring peace, but a sword.

So whether you like it or not—whether you want to be or not—you are in a battle. This conflict is no different than other conflicts that have faced our nation. It's not too late to fight.

This isn't about political parties or ideals. This is about right and wrong. This is about the standards set for us by the Word of God. This is about valuing freedom and the price that is paid for it because true freedom is never free.

There is no freedom without responsibility. We must stand against everything that is against Christ. We must rise up for the souls of men and declare righteousness and be willing to engage conflict—even physical. We're here right now for such a time as this. Souls are at stake.

So stop trying to be comfortable. Be vocal. Vote. Honor those that have stood up for righteousness. Take a stand for our freedoms in our homes. Don't be afraid of being politically incorrect. Stop shying away from conflict so you can be liked. Embrace and honor the Word of God and its righteous standards for life.

The Lie About Job

If you know anything about the Word of God, you've probably heard about Job and his boils and what God did to him, right? It's a really big deal. It's a whole book of the Bible that has been used to deceive people—especially when it comes to healing—and we're going to tear it apart.

In the first chapter of Job we learn that he was a very wealthy man. We're told that his sons took turns hosting feasts in their homes and that Job regularly offered sacrifices on behalf of his children. Then we see that Satan came to God and they talked about Job. God said there was none on earth like Job, but Satan disagreed.

Before I go into this further, let's look at Luke 22:31. Jesus tells Peter that Satan has asked to sift him as wheat, but that He prayed for him so that his faith would not fail.

What does this mean and why am I throwing it in right here? Well, when Satan asked to sift Peter as wheat that means he wanted to have dominion over him. That's what Satan was going to God for when they were talking about Job. Satan wanted dominion over Job. He thought it was unfair that God had put a hedge of protection around him. He pretty much told God, "Why wouldn't he serve you? Look at what you've done for him! If you'd allow pressure to come against him we'd really see where his heart is."

And then we see where the first lie about the character of God is pulled from. It does appear that God allowed Satan to harm Job, but that's not true. God didn't have a choice. Satan had every right to go to God and complain, and he had every right to Job. Adam gave Satan dominion over the affairs of men back in Genesis chapter 3. In Luke chapter 4 we find these words.

Luke 4:5-7

> **The devil led him up to a high place and showed him in an instant all the kingdoms of the world. And he said to him, "I will give you all their authority and splendor, <u>for it has been given to me, and I can give it to anyone I want to.</u> So if you worship me, it will all be yours."**

So we see in the earth realm, Satan has legal dominion over the kingdom of men. And because there was no intercessor at that time—there was no Jesus—Satan had a legal right to Job. God couldn't say no. So Job lost his provision and he lost his children. And here is another scripture used to deceive people about the character of God. Yes, Job lost his children, but he didn't lose his own life and he didn't lose his wife. Why did he lose his children? Well, think about it. Why do you think he offered sacrifices for them continuously? He knew there were some things going on in their lives that weren't right and he was fearful for them. We get confirmation of this later in Job—his children paid the penalty of sin.

We see another lie about the character of God in Job 1:21 when Job said, "The Lord gave and the Lord has taken away." People actually quote this today! In fact, there is a popular song that sings this and it grieves me every time I hear it. Just because something is written in the Bible doesn't mean it's proper; it just happened. We need to look at the person we're quoting and really make sure they have a proper perception of God.

Job didn't have the right perception. He lacked knowledge of the character of God. He lived in fear and gave offerings out of fear. His perception was that God gives and takes away. That was his understanding, but that is NOT God. Think about how great that sounds. Doesn't that make you want to serve God? He gives and takes away? Wow. Thanks! I can do that myself! It's a phrase you hear often, but that doesn't mean it's truth. That is where Job was. That was his perception.

Back to the Bible—Satan comes back to God and tells God Job isn't as righteous as he appears and he wants to be able to touch his body. God has to say yes, and Job develops boils. Then we begin to hear some stuff happening. We really start to see Job's heart.

In 3:25 Job says what he has feared has come upon him. And there it is. Job didn't have peace before. He was consumed with doing things right and giving offerings and trying to do things religiously correct. He wasn't in a place of knowing God's character. He was afraid of God. He dreaded these things happening. He gave offerings in his limited knowledge just to appease God.

When his friends came along to talk to him about his heart and his understanding, Job went on a tangent of severe and serious misrepresentations of God. He said God destroys both the blameless and the wicked. Do you see anything wrong with that? I do. Job had a completely wrong picture of who God is. If this was what you thought of God, what would you do? You'd give offerings everyday all day long. If this was the God you were serving you would think you have to appease him nonstop. If this is the kind of justice God has then you have to continually perform, right? Job had God all wrong.

Now let's jump to where God starts talking to Job and dealing with his perception. God shows him the goodness of creation—His goodness, His faithfulness and what He's done. God taught Job about Himself and Job finally saw that God is good.

Then Job replied to the Lord:

Job 42:2-6

> **I know that you can do all things; no plan of yours can be thwarted.**

> **You asked, "Who is this that obscures my counsel without knowledge?" Surely I spoke of things I did not understand, things too wonderful for me to know. You said, "Listen now, and I will speak; I will question you, and you shall answer me." My ears had heard of you but now my eyes have seen you. Therefore I despise myself and repent in dust and ashes.**

Then he repented—from his wrong perception of God, his wrong image of God: a works, fear-based, religious mentality of God, which gave the enemy access to his life. And God blessed Job more than ever before. So, have you believed a lie about the Book of Job? Do you know why those things happened? Do you know the end of the story? Get your Bible and read the whole thing. See what you learn. Then ask yourself if it was God's will to bring destruction to Job's life. Ask yourself if it's God's will to bring destruction—to bring sickness—to your life.

The Bible says that what God was able to bring about was a good thing. God was faithful to bring wisdom and knowledge to Job. He kept him from incurring destruction.

Job had the victory in the end. And so can you.

The Power of Family Agreement

Everything that God will do in the earth will come through a family, a husband and wife following a God-given vision while at the same time leading their children by example. Raising the next generation to serve the Lord is a very serious issue to our Father. Paul tells Timothy in 1 Timothy 3 that knowing how to lead and train our children is a prerequisite for promotion in God's Kingdom. Sadly, in recent years the church has put more emphasis on ministry than family. I know personally of many families that have collapsed while being involved on the ministry treadmill. Being in ministry myself, I know just how intense that treadmill can be. If I don't keep my family first in my day planner, they will get crowded out by many good but inappropriate activities.

We are reading headlines every day of ministry leaders whose families are being torn apart by wrong priorities. This is not the will of the Lord, and divorce is one thing that God says He hates. As children of the light, we are not ignorant of Satan's schemes, and through the power of the Holy Spirit we can win in life in every area, especially in family life.

For Drenda and me, our family is our greatest comfort and asset. Our family is whole, healthy and intact. Most visitors that come to our church are impressed, first of all, by our family. They see that we are real and not some kind of show but that we live what we preach, and we have the fruit that bears witness to that. As I shared earlier, all of my children are totally involved in the ministry. Over the years, I have never had to tell them to go to church or to force them to serve God. In fact, I am always reminding them to maintain balance, urging them not to spend every waking moment at church and in ministry work. But they just love the ministry, and that, my friend, is not an accident. It is their passion and they have the passion they have because of their upbringing.

Decide today to serve God as a family. I believe that God calls families to an assignment and as you say yes to God, you will find the passion of your life.

There are several factors that I believe have impacted my family in a positive way over the years and that have produced the fruit that I see in my children today. First of all, they saw the Word of God work as they grew up. They saw the Word of God heal our bodies, bring us out of debt, promote us in the affairs of life; and they saw many, many testimonies that bore witness to the power of our God and His Kingdom. They know God is good not only through Bible stories but also in their real lives. Why would they ever want to leave God's house?

Secondly, they saw an example of a husband and wife who loved each other, are committed to each other, and continually say yes to God in bigger and bigger assignments. And, more importantly, they see those assignments come to completion with much fruit. They know all about the pressure, the impossible odds that we faced, and they remember the times of prayer where as a family we came into agreement and saw the hand of God come through again and again.

As you may or may not know, we run at a very fast pace, more like a sprint than a run. The only way that our family stays intact is that we all run together with a common vision. There is nothing more powerful then a family that is aligned together with God's vision, in unity and running together in life. It just does not get any better than that. Mom and Dad, you cannot legalize your children's passion for God, but you can set such an example of victory in every area of life that they will desire to follow the same success that you have demonstrated to them.

Decide today to serve God as a family. I believe that God calls families to an assignment and as you say yes to God, you will find the passion of your life. When you stand where I am today and see all your children around you serving God, you will agree with me in saying that there is no amount of money that I would trade for the joy of serving God as a family!

The Power of Remembrance

It's important that we look at history—our history—in order to move forward. See, sometimes you have to remind yourself of where you've been in order to have the victory where you are now. Okay Gary, you say, you're getting all sentimental on me. Maybe I am, but this is also straight from the Word of God.

Look at Mark 8:14. The disciples had forgotten to bring bread. Then Jesus started talking about leaven and they thought He was saying that because they had forgotten to bring bread on their trip. Jesus knew that they had forgotten to bring bread, but Jesus knew that was not going to be an issue. He also knew it would be a good time to teach His disciples an important lesson. He said, "Why are you concerned about not bringing bread; don't you remember?" Then He went on to remind them of the time that He had multiplied the bread for 5,000 men and then again for 4,000 men. Apparently their victory—the answer to their fear and the issue they were facing—was in their remembering.

So Jesus walked them through the past events. He wanted them to remember the past victories and analyze the results that came from those victories, because once you learn how the Kingdom works, the lessons learned become blocks in your foundation that you will need to build on in the future.

David is another perfect example. Look at 1 Samuel 17:33. David went to battle against Goliath, but Saul told him he was just a boy and couldn't do it. Then look at what David did—he remembered. He had had previous experiences—previous victories—that allowed him to see the problem as an opportunity. He told Saul he had protected his sheep against the lion and the bear. Then look at verse 37. It's very important. David said, "The Lord who delivered me from the paw of the lion and the paw of the bear will deliver me from the hand of this Philistine." David was confident that the same God who delivered him out of those situations would deliver him out of this situation, too.

That's the power of looking back. It's vital that we develop that kind of thinking. How? Well, let me share my story.

I was called into the ministry at the age of 19. It happened at my own birthday party. A big party had been prepared, steaks and all. As I was about to take my first bite of steak, the Holy Spirit fell in that place. I looked at my unsaved friends who were looking at me and I got up and went outside. There I had a vision of me teaching people in folding chairs, and God told me I was called to preach. I didn't really know what that meant, but it launched my journey.

Next, I felt that the Lord told me to go to Oral Robert's University, which I did. There I met the best thing that has ever happened to me—my wife, Drenda. We got married and God called us into business. Wow, I had a lot to learn about life, and looking back, I can see why God led me into business before He led me into ministry. I was an idiot.

We struggled with all kinds of debt, and we learned all kinds of lessons. The key here is that *we learned*. We learned about the Kingdom and finally began to figure out how life is supposed to work. We got out of debt. We worked on our marriage. We learned how to be godly parents.

Finally in the summer of 1995, 21 years after that first vision, the Holy Spirit engulfed me in church one morning, and I knew I was called to start pastoring a church. I was 40 years old by then. I had just completed a 21-year Holy Spirit training program—and I needed it.

There are seasons and times that God has set up. He gives you a glimpse—He gives you visions and dreams—but it's not necessarily the time to step out. So there I was 21 years later, stepping out on the vision I had when I was young.

So we started a Bible study with maybe 20 people. We were able to meet in a room at a local radio station for free. The first night we met, I looked up in worship and recognized the picture instantly. It was the same picture that I saw the night I was called to preach as a teen. It was all exactly as the vision had been!

That vision now gave me confidence that I was going to be all right. I was right where God wanted me to be.

If you're going to do anything great in your life there is going to be pressure. You'll have to make tough decisions. So train yourself. Learn how faithful God is. Learn His principles. Keep prayer journals and testimonies. Hold onto mementos. Rehearse memories and victories every chance you get. Reflect. Practice the art of remembering God's faithfulness, and it will launch you into your next victory.

The Power of YOU and GOD Together

We are currently living in times that are uncharted, and honestly, there are some scary things out there right now. It's difficult to turn on the TV, read the paper or even listen to the radio without hearing a negative report. It's times like these that you have to guard your heart and stay focused on the plan and purpose that God has for you. No matter the turmoil around you, the trial you may be facing or the situation you may be in, you have to stay steadfast, knowing that, ultimately, God's plan can and will win out. His plan is to bring good to your life in ALL areas so that you may reach your full destiny. And there is power in your destiny because there is power in you!

I remember in my own life when I was facing some impossible situations, situations where God had to show up or else! There was the time when the Lord told me to launch the television ministry of *Faith Life Now* several years ago, on top of pastoring a church and leading a corporation. When the time came to sign the contract for our first season of taping, I did not know where the resources would come from, but the Lord simply told me to trust Him.

So, I moved forward in FAITH believing God for the provision. As I took one step of faith, He provided the strength and resources for the second step. As I moved forward, God provided; as I took a step, God provided; as I trusted in Him, God provided! Every single time there was a need God was right on time. He confirmed His plan to me over and over again.

If I had looked at my circumstances in the natural, there would have been no way for me to see how it could have worked. BUT GOD! I am reminded what Acts 17:26 says, "From one man he made every nation of men…and He determined the times set for them and the exact places where they should live."

The God who made heaven and earth made you with an exact moment of time in mind and an exact place, a strategic location, picked out according to your destiny. He has equipped you with everything you need to fulfill your destiny, regardless of the situation around you. Remember, you are not subject to the environment; the environment should be subject to you!

<u>God did not call us to be the thermometer; He called us to be the thermostat!</u>

There is a reason you are living in this day and age. You play a vital part of God's solution to the challenges that we face ahead. People ask me, "What can one person possibly do?" We underestimate the power of one, the potential that lies in a single life totally submitted to God's plan. Now more than ever, the world needs you to be an example of a new Kingdom, in which there's unlimited potential and freedom!

Decide today to be God's representative wherever God has placed you!

The Price of Destiny

On July 4, 1776, 56 men signed the Declaration of Independence. When they chose to sign that document, they were committing high treason, with a penalty of hanging. Later, 5 of them were captured, 12 of them had their homes seized by the British and 17 lost all that they had. Although 120,000 later joined their cause, they started as a small group of freedom fighters. In total, 26,000 died in the fight to birth the great nation of America.

These guys were heroes. Not the kind of heroes our confused culture thinks of. Sports stars aren't heroes. They change teams for better contracts. These guys were real people who put the needs of others ahead of their own. For them, there was no turning back. They were willing to pay any price. They were willing to sacrifice everything.

Butch was another hero. You probably haven't heard of him, but you'll recognize his name. Butch was a commander fighter pilot assigned to the aircraft carrier Lexington in WWII. As he took off for an attack, he realized his gas tanks hadn't been filled. When he turned back to return to the fleet, he saw a Japanese squadron heading that way. There was no one there to help. The planes had taken off and Butch had no way to reach them. He was it.

At that moment, he laid aside all thoughts of personal safety and charged forward, attacking as many enemy planes as possible. When his ammunition was gone, he dove in, trying to clip the wings or tails in the hopes of rendering them unfit to fly. Finally, the exasperated Japanese took off in another direction. When Butch landed back on the carrier and they pulled his gun cameras, they found out he had shot down five enemy aircraft and literally saved the fleet. His hometown wanted to be sure that the memory of this hero lived on, so they named an airport after him—O'Hare— the Chicago O'Hare International Airport.

> *Here's the key. A puzzle piece is unique. So are you. Now, when you take a puzzle piece and snap it into a puzzle, what happens? IT DISAPPEARS. That's God's plan for how we fit, too.*

Now, you're not necessarily called into gunfire, but what price are you willing to pay? Would you head into the conflict like Butch O'Hare? Would you be willing to take on Goliath like David? Would you be willing to give everything?

See, too many people think their destiny is free, or that it's just something God works out, but that's not true. We have to jump into the conflict. We have to work with God, and there's a price.

Matthew 13:44 tells us that the Kingdom of heaven is like treasure hidden in a field. That treasure will cost you everything.

Now, I know what you're thinking—it didn't cost David everything. He came out victorious. But David was willing to give everything to face Goliath. The promise of reward was available to King Saul and the whole army, but they were in the back quaking in fear. David was the only one willing to lay down his life for the nation and the reward.

In 1 Corinthians 6:19, we uncover the real mystery of water baptism. It says you voluntarily die to yourself. You go under water dying to self and commit to living a new life when you come up. Jesus told us to pick up our crosses daily and follow Him. What does that mean? You sacrifice everything.

If we're dead to ourselves we submit to authorities, we hold our tongue, we stop thinking we need to share our opinions and we don't bother getting offended. So, God pokes us with things we don't want to do, or uses someone who pushes our buttons, to see if we're sold out. If not, we get to pass that test again.

Here's the key. A puzzle piece is unique. So are you. Now, when you take a puzzle piece and snap it into a puzzle, what happens? IT DISAPPEARS. That's God's plan for how we fit, too. He doesn't ask us to lay down our lives because He's a hard taskmaster. He asks us to lay down our lives because He knows the bigger plan. He sees how we fit into the bigger picture.

Trust me. The puny plans you have for your life are nothing compared to God's great plans for you—plans for wealth, contentment, protection and peace. You'll have stories of you and God being heroes together, amazing stories to tell your grandkids about years from now. But there is a price. It's everything.

The Sabbath Rest

Hebrews 4:9a

There remains, then, a Sabbath-rest for the people of God.

Do you know that God wants you to have money just as bad as you do? God's plan was that the earth would be created with all the resources in it that man would ever need before man would be placed here. It took six days for God to prepare the earth and finish it for man. Man was created at the end of the sixth day of creation and God rested on the seventh day. He rested because everything was finished, not because He was tired.

God had designed creation so that man could live and exist in the seventh day with Him, and *without worry for his provision.* But, when Adam sinned, he gave that provision away. Adam's sin caused mankind to become survivalists—eking out an existence by our own labor, sweat and pain. However, God gave man a picture of what He would someday restore—the seventh day, the day of rest, the Sabbath.

On the Sabbath day man was not allowed to work, or to sweat or toil for provision. Instead, he was to REST on the Sabbath day. This was made possible by a double portion he received on the sixth day. This double portion was just as the name implied—double the amount it took to live on for one day. So, on the sixth day, man received the provision he would need to rest on the seventh day. So now you're thinking, "Wouldn't it be great if that was possible today?" Well, the great news is that it's not only possible, but it's what Jesus paid for.

When Jesus said on the cross, "It is finished," He was referring to the same finished work that God was referring to when He said it was finished back in Genesis 2, meaning that everything was now available for man and he was free from the earth-curse system of lack and poverty. Second Peter 1:3 confirms this for us when it says that we have now received everything we need for life and godliness.

God had designed creation so that man could live and exist in the seventh day with Him, and without worry for his provision.

So what does this really mean? Well, the way this thing looks in the natural world is that we now have the ability to gather and produce wealth supernaturally. We have the ability to gather and produce the double portion! This happens through God-given ideas, direction and timing. As we listen to God, He will direct us to harvest ideas and concepts that we were not aware of previously. It's this flow of ideas and new concepts that God will use to transform our lives. Remember, the Sabbath was only possible in the Old Testament by having the ability to harvest more than enough—the double portion. Hebrews 4:9 and Isaiah 61 tell us that the double portion and the Sabbath rest are available to us as the New Testament Church.

The Steps to Change

It's unbelievable what starts to happen when things get aligned properly in our families.

God wants you to prosper. And prospering starts with your family. Everything comes out of family—everything begins with family. The greatest joys—or the greatest sorrows—come out of your marriage, your children—your family. You can get everything else right, but if things aren't right in your family that's the greatest sorrow there is.

It's worth it to fix your family. But it takes work. There is a price involved. It may take some time, but it's worth it. So how do you get there? How do you move from where you're at to where you want to go? How do you get your family there?

Look with me at Judges 6 and the story of Gideon.

Gideon was an Israelite. The Israelites had done evil in the sight of God and He had turned them over to the hand of their enemy—the Midianites—for seven years. The Israelites had resorted to living in caves in the mountains. They were in survival mode. They were impoverished and oppressed, and, finally, they cried out to God.

That's the first step to change—recognize where you are and cry out to God.

It's amazing how many people put up with living in lack and with dysfunction. If we don't recognize where we're at, we can't recognize it's not where God wants us. We have to stop accepting dysfunction as normal. We need to realize that marriages are supposed to work; families don't have to scream and yell at each other. But we can't get ourselves there. We have to ask God for help.

So the Israelites did ask God for help, and He sent a prophet who told the people that they hadn't listened to the Lord.

And there's the next step to change—LISTEN for the voice of God. Listen for the answers.

If you're going to change things, you're going to have to trust God with your whole heart. We can't lean to our normal understanding anymore. We need new direction. I like to say that acknowledging God is like being at a committee meeting and someone says, "I'd like to acknowledge the gentleman in the back in the red sweater." What happens? He stands up and he speaks, and everyone listens. God has to be the man in the red sweater for us.

Now, we get to Gideon. Gideon was in a wine press hiding wheat. He had learned a system of survival; his decisions were all made around survival. There was no real freedom. He was oppressed and impoverished. He wasn't where he was supposed to be. He had learned to cope. The people knew the promises of God, but they weren't living it. So the Angel of the Lord came and spoke to Gideon.

Gideon was the smallest in his family, and his family was the smallest in the clan. But the Angel of the Lord said he was a mighty warrior and told him to, "Go in the strength you have."

Now, I'd like to talk about men for just a se cond. Men, we need to make a decision to go in the strength we have. We need to stop the deception that says we can never be a success. We need to be men who call the family prayer meeting, who stop having our wives call all the spiritual shots. Because we're the priests and the heads of our families. Our families are never going someplace we don't go.

You say you don't know why your wife is so frustrated all the time? I'll tell you why she's frustrated—because she's linked up with you. Where are you going, bud? If you don't think you're going to be a success, what are you leaving her with? She's going to be with you. Did you ever think she just might not like the direction she thinks you're going? Many times she has a higher vision for your family than you do. She's called of God to help. She's the one with the heart for the family, and for you. She wants to see the family win.

Women are amazing creatures created by God and they will adapt to everything—but failure. They don't like when men lose sight of purpose. It cuts off their very function. They're called to help with the common vision for the family, but when their man starts playing softball five nights a week, or he begins to shut down with no vision, they can't help but be frustrated.

So we need to come into agreement with God and say, "My family can have that. My family can be successful." Because God has called us to be the men. We are called by God with an anointing to lead. You have offices—they're called the husband and the father. You have an anointing to carry out those offices. It's not tied to who you are in the flesh. It's tied to who you are with God. God wants to lead you. Now, I know it can be scary.

And this is where I need to talk about women. Ladies, your husband needs a cheerleader. The Bible commands us men to lay our lives down for our wives, but He also commands wives—commands them—to respect their husbands. Your husband's number one need is not to satisfy his sexual drive, but it's for respect; for you to say, "Honey, I know you can do it. I believe in you."

He needs to come home to his own cheering section. I know. You may be saying, "You've got to be nuts! You don't know my husband! He's not worthy of respect." It doesn't matter. Is God worthy of respect? The Bible commands you to respect your husband. We need to function as God has commanded us to function in marriage and then things will begin to change.

Now, back to men.

Men need to understand that they are pastors—they are shepherds. We are all pastors, protectors, providers and leaders of our homes. We have to understand that our families are going where we're going.

God told Gideon to tear down his father's altar to Baal. Now, that was a big deal for Gideon. The whole town would see that—his family would see that. But notice that God didn't tell him to take on the whole army. He told him to tear down his wrong priorities. Men, we need to have a constant, vigilant look on our families and to tear down the wrong things in our hearts and our homes. Anything that's not prospering us or is deceiving us needs to be destroyed. We need to reestablish our hearts.

So, the next step to change is to realign and reestablish your foundation. Reestablish God as the head of your family, your finances—your life.

Once Gideon tore those things down, he was positioned. Then the Spirit of the Lord came upon him. See, it's never God's intention that you have to do this yourself. God has a plan. You just need to posture yourself so that you can receive the anointing. Get your home right and get your heart right so that, when you face the battle, the anointing of God will come upon you and give you the victory.

> *Say you're sorry. Forgive. Pray. Come into agreement with your husband or wife. It's the most powerful thing you can do.*

And that's step four to change—rely on God. He will give you the vision and strength to start.

In Judges 7:19 we see that with the anointing comes a plan. It will work that same way for you, too. You'll receive a download of strategy to move your family forward once you're positioned. And if you notice—how many men did Gideon have to actually engage in battle? None. God will do the same thing for you. It's not based on what you think your potential is. One idea at the right time can launch you into a place that you never thought you'd be.

And that's step five to change—remain in God. Every Israelite man "stood his place," and the Midianites ran. We later read that Midian was subdued and did not raise its head again. There was peace and success.

Today, I'm challenging you as a family to get the family thing right—to get the marriage thing right. Get it right and get postured for God to use you—to be a success. It can happen! God is no respecter of persons. He's already given you all things that pertain to life and godliness.

So, men, recommit your foundations. Reevaluate where you're taking your family. Drive your family toward the destination—toward the inheritance. Stop being satisfied with living the average and the ordinary. See a picture in God's Word of the future you want for your kids, and your family. Start leading. Stop following. Know you can trust God to lead you in your weakness. Remember, God told Gideon to go in the strength he had.

Say you're sorry. Forgive. Pray. Come into agreement with your husband or wife. It's the most powerful thing you can do. If you're single, come into agreement with Him. Take communion with your family. Tear down the altars to the things that are holding you back.

Then take it to the next level. Mentor a younger man or woman, or seek out mentorship if you're younger. Be humble enough to receive mentorship and training, or be generous enough to give it.

Don't limit yourself. Don't watch life. Really live it.

The Whole Being

It's time to talk about how we take care of (or don't take care of) our bodies.

As Christians, we're guilty of focusing only on the spiritual side of things and neglecting our physical bodies. We can't do that. We're made up of three parts—the spirit, the soul and the body—and if one part is sick, the whole is sick. The Bible tells us that we need to keep our whole being blameless. Are you doing that?

Now, I'm going to tell you up front that this isn't meant to be condemnation. I'm not telling you anything that doesn't prick me, too. I've done it, too. I've eaten the wrong things, not gotten enough sleep and carried stress. We abuse our bodies. We take them for granted but we could avoid a whole lot of sickness and disease if we would just take care of ourselves.

See, God says our bodies are not our own. He gave us the responsibility of caring for them—of presenting them to Him the best we can. He gives us plenty of scriptures to remind us of that. First Corinthians 6:13 tells us our body is for the Lord. First Corinthians 6:19 tells us that our bodies are temples of the Holy

Spirit and that we should honor God with them. Romans 12:1 says we should be pleasing to God—our whole being should be pleasing to Him.

Oral Roberts believed this concept of the whole being. Back when I was 19, I applied to his university—ORU. I knew I didn't qualify for their minimum entrance requirements because of my 1.3 GPA. But because they had seen my record of straight A's in a Bible study course I took after I was saved, I had an opportunity to explain the change in my life—and I received a letter of acceptance with a catch. They sent me this letter telling me I didn't qualify scholastically, but that they were allowing me to attend there if I could maintain a certain degree of excellence in my studies. But what they said next shocked me. They told me I didn't qualify physically.

They told me I could come to ORU, but that when I first arrived on campus I would be weighed and, if I didn't weigh 211 pounds or less, I could not attend ORU.

At that time I weighed 235 pounds and was quickly heading toward 240. See, I worked in my dad's pizza shop. We stayed open until 1:00 a.m. and would make White Castle runs at 2:00 a.m. Mountain Dew was my beverage of choice back then. I wasn't heading for a good place physically.

How would I lose 24 pounds in 5 months? I had no training. I started running. I didn't know what I was doing, but I committed myself to the process of trying to lose weight. When I got to campus 5 months later, I weighed 209 pounds. Whew!

Then, to stay in school, you had to do a certain amount of activity. They even tracked it. It was at ORU that I really began to develop the love of running and the love of exercise. I got down to 195 pounds.

In case you're wondering, I weigh 200 now. I want to get back to 195. I want my whole body to honor God. I want to worship God with my whole being.

As believers we get stuck in the thinking that worship is just standing in church, raising your hands and singing slow songs. That is one way to worship, but worship is so much more than that. Worship is honoring God. Jesus said if we love Him we'll do what He commands. That's true worship.

> *Then throw your Twinkies at the altar of God. Start making changes slowly. Eat more veggies and more lean meats. Start exercising.*

If we love God we are going to offer our bodies as living sacrifices. We are going to recognize and remind ourselves every day that we are temples of the Holy Spirit. We are going to worship God with our lifestyles. We are going to worship Him by taking care of our bodies.

Now, don't think Satan isn't onto this. He has some schemes and tactics to devalue and destroy our temples. Because we can't fulfill our assignment if we're not healthy, and the first step to being unhealthy is not taking care of our bodies.

We need to be aware of the tactics of the enemy. We need to be aware of what we are doing to our bodies. Many of today's diseases are from ignorance or lack of self-control.

So how do you get informed? How do you make better decisions? Study what you eat! Did you know that there are more than 3,000 approved chemicals/additives in the food we eat? Did you know that many decisions in the food industry are made based on profit? Do you know what is in your food? Do you know what you're really putting in your mouth?

God wants you healthy. He wants you full of life. We have a race to run. You can't continue to neglect your body. We have to take care of our bodies to be full of life. People think they can just do what they want and have hands laid on them when they get sick—but once you're aware of this you're held accountable. You have to change what you're doing to your body.

Now, we all know change isn't easy. We're all bombarded with advertisements. We're used to convenience. We have to pray for the grace to change, for self-control, even for healing emotionally if that's where you're at.

Then throw your Twinkies at the altar of God. Start making changes slowly. Eat more veggies and more lean meats. Start exercising.

Do whatever you need to do to be able to offer your body as a living sacrifice to God.

There's a Reason You Are Here

Drenda and I went to Australia for a conference. While we were there, we had this guy named Matt who was driving us around and taking care of us. When we got done with the conference, Matt asked me if I wanted to go crab hunting with him. I didn't know anything about crab hunting, but I said sure.

Now, mud crabs are a big deal in Australia. They're $48 a piece at the store. And we needed to feed a good size group of people that night. I was in a second boat with Matt's brother, and he told me he was stretching his faith and believing for 6 crabs. I thought we needed more than that, so I told him I was believing for 15-20 of them.

We went out and caught 18 crabs.

I didn't know anything about that so I didn't think it was big deal. I found out the next day that 18 crabs was a big deal when Matt called his dad on the phone in the car and his dad went nuts on the Bluetooth yelling, "Praise God! God is good! That's unbelievable!" That's when I found out that they normally only catch 3 crabs.

Now, what do you think Matt and his brother are over there

talking about in Australia? Do you think he's talking about some religious rules and regulations? No! He's talking about the 18 crabs!

See, Mark 16:15 tells us to go into the world and share the good news of the Gospel, but we misinterpret the term *good news*. John 3:16 tells us how much He loves people and how important people are to Him, but in case you haven't noticed, John 3:16 isn't good news to the world. It doesn't mean a thing to them. What kind of good news are they looking for? Eighteen crabs instead of 3. Bills paid. House paid off.

It is important to God that people hear about the Kingdom. Yes, the Kingdom.

Not the rules and regulations and do's and don'ts of religion. The devil loves that, because no one wants to serve a God like that. He doesn't need that kind of advertisement.

And that's where you come in.

Romans 10:14 says,

> **How, then, can they call on the one they have not believed in? And how can they believe in the one of whom they have not heard? And how can they hear without someone preaching to them?**

The good news isn't religious doctrine. The good news is you. You're supposed to demonstrate what good news looks like.

Peter, James and John had fished all night and caught nothing. Then Jesus came along and said, "Uh, excuse me. Let me lease your business for awhile for the Kingdom." And they took in more fish than their boats could handle. I mean, the boats were sinking!

When Jesus said, "Come follow me," He didn't say, "If you

love God, you'll follow me." Peter, James and John didn't follow Him and say, "We're unworthy." No, they said, "We've never seen a catch like this! We're following YOU!"

That's how it is. That's what it's about.

When John the Baptist heard about Jesus, he sent his guys to find out if Jesus was the one. When they asked Jesus, He didn't say, "Yes, God sent me to condemn the world."

No, He said, "Tell John the blind eyes are open, people are healed, lepers are cleansed and good news has been preached to the poor." He was saying, "Go back and tell John we caught 18 crabs!"

That's what people want. They want to know how you caught those crabs. They want to know how your marriage is no longer falling apart, or how you got out of debt or how you aren't sick anymore. You should be demonstrating results that are different than what the world normally sees.

That is the reason you are here.

Use Your Authority!

You know, when you read the Bible you don't find Jesus praying to God to heal people. No. Jesus had been given the authority. He acted on His Father's behalf with power and demonstration.

Look at Matthew 8. Jesus went to Peter's house and saw Peter's mother-in-law lying in bed with a fever. He touched her hand and the fever left her. Then she got up and started to wait on Him.

Notice that it doesn't say that Jesus called a prayer meeting with the church staff. It doesn't say that He called for everyone to go on a 55-day fast. No. It says Jesus touched her and she was healed.

Jesus healed all of the sick this way. He decreed it so and it was so. You won't find any scriptures where Jesus was saying, "God, please do this." He drove demons out. He drove them out with a word, not a prayer.

And you know what? God's plan was to have a whole body of believers out there doing the same things Jesus did. His plan was to have YOU out there doing the same things Jesus did! Second Corinthians 5 says that you're the ambassador of the Kingdom of God. Ephesians 2:6 tells us that God raised us up with Christ.

Pay close attention to this scripture. If God raised us up with Jesus and seated us with Him, then you are seated at the Father's right hand. Since you are seated, you must be on the throne. That infers kingship and authority. YOU HAVE BEEN GIVEN THE SAME AUTHORITY AS JESUS.

And you have a mighty government that backs you. Just like a sheriff who can pull over a semi-truck many times his size because he has a badge, you have authority. You have the Kingdom of God backing you.

So, when you speak in agreement with heaven, all heaven beckons to carry it out. This is why the Bible teaches us about the power of our words. When you speak in agreement with heaven, the devil can't tell you apart from Jesus.

If you really got this, you wouldn't just be surviving life. You would be kicking the devil's butt! You should be! You should be reigning in life and demonstrating authority. But you have to stop buying into the enemy's lies. You have to stop thinking that God is holding out on you. Enough is enough! Satan doesn't want you to know who you really are and it's worked! He has deceived you into thinking you have no authority in your life.

Why are you putting up with this stuff? SAY SOMETHING! Tell him to stop! Take authority! Stop talking about what the enemy is doing to you and start talking about what you are doing to him!

The world is crying out for justice. People want heroes. That's YOU!

Will you decree it? Will you speak up? Will you enforce God's justice in the earth realm and make a difference in your life and in the lives around you?

There's Gold in There

Here's an interesting story. In 1799, the owners of the Reed Farm in Raleigh, North Carolina found a big rock on their property. They thought it made a great doorstop. Now, keep in mind that gold mining was the second largest business venture after agriculture at that time. So, for 3 years these people used this big rock as a doorstop until, one night, a local jeweler came over for dinner. He saw the rock and checked it out. It was a 17-pound nugget of 24-carat gold!

Yes, this is a true story. Later, they found other nuggets on that farm. In fact, by 1831 they had found more than $10 million worth of gold. Ten million dollars! Now, you tell me—how many times do you think those people had walked around that gold nugget doorstop? How many times do you think they moved it in and out of place never knowing what they had their hands on? In fact, according to the story, they sold that rock for pretty cheap. You know that jeweler wasn't about to tell them what that rock was when he bought it from them.

So why am I telling you that story? Because your ideas are just like that rock. The Kingdom in you is just like that rock. And you're probably just like those people on the farm. Maybe you're walking around it not knowing it's there, or you're bumping into it and moving it around every day and you still haven't realized it. Let me tell you, it is the most valuable thing you possess! Maybe you do realize that fact a little, but you don't know what to do with it or how to move forward.

First, you need to understand how the Kingdom of God operates. Then, you need to get a God-breathed dream on the inside of you. Having that dream will get you out of bed in the morning. It will motivate you and pull you. It will be all you can talk about. It will change your life.

Remember, your dream may look like someone else's problem. I always say, "If you see a problem, you can solve it, because you recognize it." Many times, people don't recognize a problem, or they put up with it because they've become accustomed to it. Or, they run from it because they don't think God's in it. But, when you see it, you can fix it. Just look at it as an opportunity. Think like David and look at the reward. As I shared earlier, 1 Samuel 17 records that David came with the supplies and heard Goliath ranting and raving. He said 3 times in that chapter—you can go check it out—3 times, he said, "What will be done for the man who rids Israel of this disgrace? What will be done?" They told him the reward, and he asked again. In fact, his brother got annoyed with him for asking. But what was on David's mind? The reward.

So start looking for your reward. When you find your opportunity, ask God for the plan to walk it out. It's time to make it happen.

God has put gold on your farm. It's time to see it.

Wanted: People Who Seek Their Destinies

So you want to find your place in this life. You want to find your destiny. But all you see is the chain store or the fast food joint or the call center you work in, and you want to run. But let me tell you something that most people in our instant culture don't want to accept—you have to be obedient one day at a time.

We live in a culture where you can microwave your dinner, or hit a drive-through and "have it your way." You can reach almost anyone almost anywhere at almost any time by pressing a button on your phone. So people want instant results all the time, and when they don't get the results that they want, they get disillusioned and they bail. But that's the world's system, not God's.

God has a system in place to change us, to mature us and to train us. Hebrew 12:5 tells us that God disciplines the ones He loves and He chastens everyone He accepts as His sons. Of course, no discipline seems pleasant at the time, but to discover your destiny, it's necessary. There WILL be some uncomfortable days in God's training system. He isn't always going to call you into training in the things you like. There is no training in that. You can want to ride the horses all you want, but for now you have to clean the stalls. In our culture, that respect and honor for paying a price is just about gone, and God can't use us that way.

You're the puzzle piece that fits into His big picture after all, so He's going to work with you to take the edges off. Those edges need smoothed so that when you fit in your place, it's going to feel so comfortable you'll never want to leave. Of course, there will be pain with it, but it's worth the pursuit. I was being trained from the time I was called to preach when I was 19 to when I started the church at 40. I was being trained with pain and humbleness and weeping and gnashing of teeth. That's what I was doing! But it was worth it! It's worth it.

Look at Exodus. God saw the suffering of His people and He had come to rescue them. He made some great promises, but there was some training that needed to take place. Just like us, the Israelites said, "Sign me up!" but they didn't want to deal with the tough part—the training.

> *So, don't quit. Stay on the Potter's wheel. Don't run back to Egypt. Stay where God calls you until He speaks again.*

Instead of leading the Israelites on the road through the Philistine country, God led them around it. He knew they couldn't handle war. God knew them. He knew if they were to face that kind of pressure, they might change their minds and head back to Egypt. He knows you, too. He knows the kind of pressure you can handle and the kind of pressure that will make you cave. He has a plan. He has a very detailed strategy.

David had battled the lion and the bear before he battled Goliath. The Israelites faced the Red Sea. Then, in the wilderness, God provided for them every day, but He was testing them to see if they would follow His instructions. Because, at the River Jordan, they had to know how to hear God and follow His very detailed instructions. But they faced the River Jordan and they backed down. They hadn't overcome their slave mentality. They hadn't changed in their hearts.

If you tell a child to go clean their room and they stomp their feet, huff and puff and slam the door, it doesn't matter if they clean the room or not, their heart was rebellious. Someday, they will leave home and the legality that was holding their heart back will be lifted and their heart will have the freedom to express itself. Then, you have a problem on your hands.

Instead of trying to find results outside of ourselves, and trying to get quick fixes, we should be trying to fix ourselves— to fix our hearts. Only God can do that. He has to change us to enable us to occupy what we envision. See, people will say that they've been "called" to something, or that they've been praying for this opportunity. Sure, they say that on the front end. Then they get involved, and they find out it's not easy, that it takes real work. We can try to bypass God's system all we want, but we'll never embrace our destiny.

So, don't quit. Stay on the Potter's wheel. Don't run back to Egypt. Stay where God calls you until He speaks again. (There were days in my life that I begged Him to speak to me, to do anything rather than what I was doing. But all He said was, "Stay there, keep going.") Stick it out. Take the time to be trained, mentored and sent out with wisdom. Submit to the system. Say yes whether you like it or not. Just say yes to God. He'll make something of your life that is amazing.

Watch Your Mouth

"This job is killing me!"

"I don't think we're ever going to get ahead."

"I'll just be on medication for the rest of my life."

Take a few minutes to think about what has come out of your mouth in the last 24 hours.

Now, what if I told you that your words hold the same power as God's?

I've shared about justice and the Kingdom of God. Romans 10:10 says, "For it is with your heart that you believe and are justified, and it is with your mouth that you confess and are saved." This is a powerful principle. When our heart agrees with heaven then we are justified, that means we have given heaven legality in our lives. However, nothing happens yet because we have jurisdiction here in the earth realm. So when we believe in our heart then everything is legal, heaven awaits its orders. Then comes the next part: we confess and are saved. Notice we confess then heaven is actually released. Do you see it? Your words are what heaven binds or looses. You have the keys of the Kingdom here in the earth realm. There is a lot of responsibility in having that authority.

Revelation 1 tells us we are kings and priests here in the earth realm on behalf of the Kingdom of God. In other words, we have the authority and the anointing to carry out the work of enforcing justice and the anointing of healing that the world so desperately needs.

Step back and think about what you're saying. Don't say, "Well, I've tried that 'faith stuff' but it hasn't worked." Don't say you don't trust God, or you're not seeing results. Make sure that you're not decreeing junk! Remember, Jesus killed a fig tree with His words of authority and brought Lazarus out of the grave with that same authority. The funny thing about Christians is that they think that when they pray that God all of a sudden says, "Stop everyone, so and so is praying, I need to hear what they are saying." No, the fact is you have been speaking all the time, not just when you pray. This is why Jesus says in Mark 11:24, "Therefore...whatever you ask for in prayer, believe you have received it, and it will be yours." A few verses before this He explains how the fig tree was killed by the power of words. Then He says, "Therefore."

Do you see it? Our petitions, our words, have authority; they can kill or bring life. When we bring a petition before heaven most people think it means we are asking God for something. No, that is not the case. Second Peter 1:3 says we have been given all things that pertain to life and godliness (or righteousness). So we are not asking as we think in the terms of asking. Instead, we are making a requisition of something that we already have! We are laying claim to what we need, not asking God, hoping He will maybe answer. No, we already have the authority, the position, the office.

See, it doesn't matter if you go to church and sing and say, "In Jesus' name." What are you saying at 3:00 a.m. when they're coming the next day to shut off your electric? What are you saying about that sickness? What are you decreeing and declaring about your life?

Proverb 18:21 says that our words have the power of life and death.

You HAVE to be careful. You will walk in EXACTLY what you decree. God gave YOU the keys. The authority is in YOUR hands. James 3 tells us that we are setting the course of our lives with our words, but most people have no clue how this works. They're trying to get to one place and end up somewhere else, and they wonder why. It's like setting out for London and ending up in the Philippines. You're the one steering the ship. If you end up shipwrecked on shores you didn't intend to go to, it's because you decreed it.

The Bible tells us that we have the crown and that we are seated with Christ in heavenly places. But with that authority comes responsibility. The Bible also tells us that we will have to give an account for every careless word we have spoken. Why? Because God has seated us with Christ in heavenly places and our words are binding. We are ruling on behalf of the King and will be held accountable for what we have decreed.

That's a sobering thought, but it's meant to be positive. Think of what you can decree! Don't fear that authority. Rejoice in it. Speak the good things. Say "yes" and "amen" to every promise. Decree provision, healing, direction, wisdom and health. Use your words wisely.

What Are You Thinking?

You've heard the stories and I know you've wondered. What makes a person have an affair? Why would someone who was created as a man decide he wants to be a woman? Why are people putting their Bibles down and walking away from church? What causes *any* person to be willing to do something that they know could destroy their reputation, their family and their business? The answer is *deception*.

To be deceived means to believe what is false to be true, to be misled or to be ensnared. We all know a few stories of deception—the woman who found out her husband had another family; the politician who was caught in a web of lies; or the older neighbor couple who got cheated out of thousands of dollars by a contractor. But did you know that the Bible says that we can deceive ourselves? I bet you don't know of anyone sharing those stories.

"How is that possible," you ask? "How can we deceive ourselves?" Pretty easily actually—we deceive ourselves with our *thoughts*.

Thoughts are not innocent. They're seeds. They're pictures. What you listen to, what you look at, the things you do, the friends you hang around all produce thoughts—pictures—in your mind whether you know it or not. When you begin to concentrate on those pictures, they produce desire and desire can get you into trouble.

Test every thought you have against God's will for you. How do you know His will? Read your Bible.

In fact, the Bible says that desire *drags* us. It produces a plan to *get* what it wants, and that plan can take you to a place you never thought you'd be. Don't get me wrong—that's a good thing if you're thinking about good things. Your good desires can drag you to succeed, and to win. The problem is that your heart can't tell the difference between a good desire and an evil desire. That's where we have to get a handle on things because this is nothing to play with—it's life and death.

So what do we do? How do we figure out if we're deceiving ourselves when deceived people don't usually even know they're deceived?

We start by being careful what we look at, what we listen to and who we talk to. This is what the Bible calls guarding our hearts. Then we make a decision to choose what we're thinking about. "That's crazy," you say? "How can we choose what we think when stuff just pops into our heads all the time?"

Well, the Bible says that we're to take captive every thought to make it obedient to Christ. Plain and simple, your brain does not have the authority to think anything it wants. You *can* choose what you think about.

Test every thought you have against God's will for you. How do you know His will? *Read your Bible*. Measure everything against what God says. Umpire your thoughts. If they don't line up with what God says, get them out—replace them with a right thought. How do you know what right thought to think? *Read your Bible*.

This is why I say that memory verses are not just for kids; they're for everyone. If you memorize some scriptures you'll have them ready and waiting to replace those negative thoughts.

When you analyze what happens in someone's story of a breakthrough, you'll almost always find the same scenario—they made a decision to change their *thoughts*. They took the time to make a change. They turned the TV off. They started really reading their Bibles. They elevated God's Word above the other voices in their lives and set their hearts on it.

How do you know what right thought to think? Read your Bible.

So are you ready for a breakthrough? Then make a decision to change your thoughts, to change your pictures. Ask yourself —"What have I been looking at? What have I been watching? How much time have I spent in the Word of God this week? Who am I listening to? Who is giving me advice? Is it someone that has failed or someone that has walked it out and can show me which way to go? What am I focusing on? What am I thinking?"

Ask yourself these questions and then you'll see your future.

What Is Your Mindset?

Mark 9:23

Everything is possible for him who believes.

Think about this for a minute—if you think you can win at something, you will gladly jump right in because you know the likely outcome, right? But, you won't even bother starting something that you don't think is possible, right? Never! That's because the earth-curse system has trained all of us to think that losing is part of life and that we shouldn't rock the boat—we should just conform and not risk too much. But, you're learning to think differently, right? You're learning that God has equipped you with the ability to win in any environment and confrontation. How? Because God is with you and His wisdom is yours.

Plenty of Christians, if not most, have a faulty idea when it comes to money. They think that God will bring the money from someplace, but they have no idea from where. What we need to understand is that the world worships money and no one is going to just hand it over. But people will pay BIG money for someone who can solve a problem they're facing, or provide them with something they need. And it's there that we find our opportunity to wade into a situation and provide a God solution.

As I shared earlier, that's just what David did when the nation of Israel was facing a terrifying situation—named Goliath. A lot was at stake. In fact, the whole nation was on the verge of being enslaved. The stakes were so high, and the situation so intimidating, that the army of Israel and their king, Saul were quaking with fear. Imagine the emotional hopelessness they must have felt. But when David came into that situation, he wasn't overwhelmed like the rest of the army was. Instead, in 1 Samuel 17:26 it says, "David asked the men standing near him, 'What will be done for the man who kills this Philistine and removes this disgrace from Israel?'" David asked this same question three times to three different men standing there. It's obvious what was consuming David's mind—the reward of the king's daughter, great wealth and his family being exempt from taxation. David was not consumed with fear. He saw it as an opportunity, not a problem, and you know the rest of the story.

When we ask God for money, He'll direct us right to an intersection into someone's problem where we have an opportunity to offer a solution. That's how promotion comes in the earth realm, and that's the way it comes in your life. The problem with most people is that they have trained themselves to try to *avoid* problems, not *look* for them. But that's exactly how your thinking must change! You can't dread the future! You need to look at it with excitement! In fact, as the world gets darker with all kinds of problems, our opportunities increase. But it all comes down to how you see the situation.

So, let me ask you—what is your mindset today? Do you see your life as half empty or half full? I encourage you to step back and look at yourself through the eyes of God. You can find out how He thinks about you in His Word. And yes, all things are possible to those that believe!

Today, find every scripture you can about what God says about your potential. Write them down and meditate on them as often as possible.

What Time Is It?

Did you see the U.S. Women's Team win the 400m relay race and set a new world record at the 2012 Summer Olympics? They shattered one of the oldest world records in the games—by .55 seconds. Yes, I said .55 seconds. Only a little more than half of a second made all the difference.

Time is important. Granted, we're not all running relay races in the Olympics against the fastest people in the world, but we are all running a race. Your race is why you're here. Acts 17:26 says,

> **From one man he made all the nations, that they should inhabit the whole earth; and he marked out their appointed times in history and the boundaries of their land.**

God determined when you would be born and where. He has a specific destiny for you—a specific race for you to run; an assignment; a purpose—and He's very serious about it. He's counting on you to run your race and to win.

But to run your race, you have to know the rules of the race; you have to know the track and the boundaries; you have to know where you're called to run. And you have to know when it's time to run.

Do you remember the story of the widow and the oil in the Bible?

2 Kings 4:1-7:

> The wife of a man from the company of the prophets cried out to Elisha, "Your servant my husband is dead, and you know that he revered the Lord. But now his creditor is coming to take my two boys as his slaves."
>
> Elisha replied to her, "How can I help you? Tell me, what do you have in your house?"
>
> "Your servant has nothing there at all," she said, "except a small jar of olive oil."
>
> Elisha said, "Go around and ask all your neighbors for empty jars. Don't ask for just a few. Then go inside and shut the door behind you and your sons. Pour oil into all the jars, and as each is filled, put it to one side."
>
> She left him and shut the door behind her and her sons. They brought the jars to her and she kept pouring. When all the jars were full, she said to her son, "Bring me another one."
>
> But he replied, "There is not a jar left." Then the oil stopped flowing.
>
> She went and told the man of God, and he said, "Go, sell the oil and pay your debts. You and your sons can live on what is left."

What's the most valuable thing in this story? Here's a hint: it wasn't the oil.

It was the time she had taken to gather the pots. If you could talk to her now and ask her what she would change if she could go back, I guarantee she would say she would have taken more time to gather more pots. If she truly understood the opportunity, she would have said, "I'll tell you what. I'll be back in 30 days." And she would have had semi-trucks of pots coming in. She would have been recorded in the Bible as being the wealthiest woman on the face of the earth!

> *Once you find out about your race, weigh all of your decisions against it. Determine what you'll do by where you're heading. Don't get lured into distraction. Understand there is a price to pay for being all God has called you to be.*

Time is valuable. It can never be recovered and especially the time of preparation.

My grandpa died when he was in his 90's. Before he died, I remember having a conversation with him where he asked, "Where did my life go?" I thought it was strange then, but now I understand. What my grandpa was saying was, "Pass me another pot!" But there were no jars left.

Have you ever noticed how the Bible says, "In the time of (person)?" Well, now the books are being written and they say, "In the time of (your name here!)" This is your time. This is your life. This is your race!

So ask God to show you what you're to do. Your pastor can't tell you how to find God's plan for your life, only God can. He will reveal it to you as you seek Him. Ask Him to show you your purpose and your goal. Until you know your purpose, you'll have no clarity. Until you know your goal, you'll have no sense of urgency.

Once you find out about your race, weigh all of your decisions against it. Determine what you'll do by where you're heading. Don't get lured into distraction. Understand there is a price to pay for being all God has called you to be.

Paul said in 1 Corinthians 9:24-27:

> **Do you not know that in a race all the runners run, but only one gets the prize? Run in such a way as to get the prize. Everyone who competes in the games goes into strict training. They do it to get a crown that will not last, but we do it to get a crown that will last forever. Therefore I do not run like someone running aimlessly; I do not fight like a boxer beating the air. No, I strike a blow to my body and make it my slave so that after I have preached to others, I myself will not be disqualified for the prize.**

You're going to have to clarify things and clean the clutter from your life. You might have to make some uncomfortable decisions. The race won't always be comfortable.

How you handle time will determine whether or not you will reach your destiny—whether or not you win your race.

What You Must Know

Have you ever played the telephone game? You might have played it as a child. One person would whisper something into someone's ear, and they would turn and whisper the sentence to the next person and so on and so on. By the time the message had passed through a dozen people it never sounded the same. It was a funny game when we were kids.

It's not so funny as an adult. It's especially not funny in the Church.

Of course, we don't actually play the game in church, Satan does. He uses versions of the telephone game—like gossip, slander, judgmental attitudes and unforgiveness—to try to hinder peoples' assignments, and to take them out prematurely. And it works.

Yes, Satan has been defeated. He's under our feet. But that isn't going to stop him from trying. Think about it. If you and I were going head to head and you had an atomic bomb and I had a firecracker, I would know my chances. So I'd have to change tactics, right? That's what Satan does. He uses intimidation and underground resistance, and he comes at us from the inside out. He doesn't knock on your door and say, "Hey! It's me." He operates in darkness.

Matthew 12:25 says, "Jesus knew their thoughts and said to them, 'Every kingdom divided against itself will be ruined, and every city or household divided against itself will not stand.'"

The enemy knows this. So he baits you. He baits you to come outside of your love walk. He baits you with offense. Offense is the most effective way the enemy pulls us out of the Kingdom.

He doesn't have to tempt us to murder someone. He doesn't have to tempt us to steal. He just has to divide us, and get us outside of love in our marriages, our families, our friendships and our church, and he's got us outside of God's legal jurisdiction.

And he's going to keep trying. He's going to set up schemes and people to pull you out of love, and he's going to try to use you to offend others. He's after your unity and your oneness. Divide and conquer. That's his greatest weapon.

In 1 Corinthians 11:17-34, Paul is teaching about the Lord's Supper. He's telling Christians that some of them are sick, weak and have died. WHY? They had a covenant of healing! They had the apostles still alive! They had Paul coaching them! Why were they sick and dying?

Let me just be plain about this; the problem was division. They weren't walking in love. It was all about them. There was jealousy and envy. Someone likely thought they were better than someone else. Many people get sick and never understand why. This is why! The enemy uses these tactics to divide us and gain access to our lives.

In 1 Corinthians 12:12-27, Paul tells us that we're all one body, and there should be no division. We have to understand that we're ONE BODY. We're a unit. We're <u>His</u> Body working together for the Kingdom.

The Bible says to "mark" those people that are being used by the enemy to cause division. God will deal with people severely if they are causing division because they are breaking the unity of His Body. He will make it known.

So don't let the enemy gain access. Work at preventing divisions in your life. Examine yourself. Recognize the Body. Stop talking to those friends who, when you get off the phone with them, you feel like you need a bath. Be very careful. Let the Holy Spirit discipline you. Ask God to help you to be quick to forgive. Overlook all offenses. Believe the best in people. Then, you'll really see the Kingdom of God operating in your life.

Where Do I Fit?

If I handed you a puzzle piece, could you tell me what it was an image of? Even if you could make out what may be on your piece, you still wouldn't have any idea how that piece fits into the bigger picture.

You're like that puzzle piece in the Body of Christ. By yourself, you don't make much sense. But when you find your place in the big picture, everything makes sense.

When you're born, you don't know your place or your purpose. There's a reason. Remember, King Herod tried to kill Jesus as a baby. The enemy would come for you in the same way if he knew your destiny. He would love to bring interference and to stop you from ever getting started. So, it's God's wisdom and in your best interest to keep the complete picture of your destiny from you until you're mature and tested enough to reach it.

I get calls from people that are in ministry and things are crashing down around them. Some of them have simply stepped out too soon. They had a vision and jumped right into it. See, in the world we get impatient. God isn't like that. He takes the time to make sure that you're ready to occupy the place that He is sending you. He wants to make sure that when you reach that intersection of time, location and purpose in your life, that you'll be able to stick a flag in the ground and claim it as His territory in the name of Jesus. He won't send you there if you're not ready.

In 1 Corinthians 3, we read a letter from Paul to a young church that is just coming into Christ and making some mistakes. In this chapter, Paul tells them that the Lord has assigned to each his task.

As people, we want to be cool. We want to fit in. We want to be like everyone else. But being a part of the crowd isn't what makes you valuable. Like gold and silver, what makes you valuable is your scarcity. There is no one else like you. God made you unique for a reason. Paul says, "The man who plants and the man who waters each have ONE task." You have one task, or purpose, that you were created for, and God will reward you based on how you handle that task.

God gave us the instructions for how to handle that task in 1 Corinthians 9:24. He told us to run our race in such a way as to get the prize. Think of how someone trains for a race. Think about how dedicated, how willing to sacrifice and how focused they are. Distractions don't pull them off their scheduled time to train. They understand the finish line. They understand the starting block. They know that the race can be won or lost in any of those moments, so they practice and practice and practice.

Training for a race isn't easy. It isn't always exciting. Finding your place isn't always exciting. There are still chores that have to be done.

Look at Luke 16. It's The Parable of the Shrewd Manager. This story is vital. It's about the chores and about promotion. See, this manager didn't do his job. But when he found out he was losing his job, he suddenly found a way to take care of things, to be diligent.

He failed the test. He wasn't working to help his master. He only worked when it helped him. That, right there, is why many Christians never reach their potential and their destiny. God can't trust them with it; they do not have a Kingdom mindset. If God would prosper them in a big way, it would be about them and it would hurt their life.

See, Christians get all excited about the anointing, but the anointing isn't what takes you to your destiny. God trains you every day. You prove you're ready to occupy your destiny by how you handle the affairs of life. Your trustworthiness over the little things, and the big things, is what moves you forward.

Have you ever gone into a fast food restaurant just before closing? Oh, that's a wonderful experience. You walk in the place and you'd swear they had closed a few hours ago. They might even have the chairs up on the tables. I went into one and the employees who were still there actually argued in front of me over who was going to wait on me. Here's the thing, in the minds of the people working there, that job didn't mean anything. It was a temporary job on the way to their destiny. That's where they failed the test. They thought they were going to reach their destiny by some ability or some talent, but in the world of the Spirit, God is the One that promotes. And whether or not you get promoted isn't about the anointing, it's about being on time, being loyal and doing what you said you would do. Those employees missed their opportunity to learn and be mentored.

Think about it, they were working in one of the most successful franchises in history. They should have been taking notes on how everything is run. They should have asked questions, hoping someday to be able to have as much impact in life as the place they worked. But they didn't. They were just waiting for the time clock to clock out. And that is how most Christians live.

God promoted David to King. But David had been on the hillside risking his life to save sheep. He loved God and his family, and he had been faithful and loyal with a trust. Joseph was in prison 13 years. He was also faithful over Potiphar's house and in the prison, and he had success. He viewed every assignment as worthy to do his best in. That is why he was promoted to second in command.

As I shared, after I had a vision that I would start preaching, God didn't tell me to start preaching. He told me to go to college. See, I had to get qualified to handle a trust. So I went to school. I didn't start preaching after college either. God told me to go sell life insurance. Now, I was a shy kid and that was hard. But God knew I had to change on the inside. Twenty-one years later, I preached my first service. Yes, I know it probably didn't have to take that long, but it did for me. There are no shortcuts with God. You can't fool Him. Your character has to be developed enough to be ready to do what you're called to do. God is a rewarder. He knows your heart. He's got to know and you've got to know that you can handle the responsibility there. He's going to find out if you can handle it there by watching what you're doing here and now, in the small things, under someone else's vision.

So, serve your employer wholeheartedly as if you were serving God. Don't complain or murmur. Prove that you can handle a trust. Ask yourself, "How can I help this place profit?" Make yourself so valuable that they can't handle the thought of you ever leaving. Be faithful where you are and watch. God will show you just where you fit.

Where Your Mind Goes

Have you ever been riding a bicycle and tried to look at something behind you? It's not easy. The old phrase "Where your eyes go, your body follows" kicks in, and you tend to steer the bike in the direction your head is turning.

That phrase is usually something that sports trainers and coaches say, but it really applies to nearly every area of your life. Because where your eyes and your mind go, your life follows; how you're approaching your life—your perspective—is affecting where you're going.

Look at Numbers 13. God told Moses to send some men to explore the land of Canaan. He sent them and they saw that the land was good. But then what happened?

Verses 31-33 tell us:

> But the men who had gone up with him said, "We can't attack those people; they are stronger than we are." And they spread among the Israelites a bad report about the land they had explored. They said, "The land we explored devours those living in it. All the people we saw there are of great size. We saw the Nephilim there

(the descendants of Anak come from the Nephilim). We seemed like grasshoppers in our own eyes, and we looked the same to them.

They had the WRONG perspective. It didn't matter that they had the promises of God; they couldn't see the promises for themselves.

So many people are living like that—focused on the wrong things and having no clue who they really are and who God created them to be. I don't know about you, but I'm tired of the Church hiding. If the Bible says it, it should be so. You don't have to accept mediocrity and failure as a way of life! You have the promises of God!

> *So many people are living like that—focused on the wrong things and having no clue who they really are and who God created them to be.*

You have the potential to create your life every day, but you have to walk out the principles; you have to engage. That might mean you have to make some hard choices.

A lot of Christians I know say they must have missed God whenever things get tough. For some reason we have this idea that if God is in it, it will easy. Be sure to note this—that is not true—no matter who told you that. God will empower you with His grace and you will overcome, but easy is not in the Bible. God wants you to stay steadfast during those times. He wants you to step up to the plate. So how do you do that? Ask yourself these three questions:

1. What am I looking at?

What's your perspective? How do you see yourself? Is it time for a change of scenery? Are you looking at the promises of God or at your problems? The Word of God should be your mirror. Your heart is going to produce what it's meditating on. Set your sights on what God says. Then protect and guard your heart.

2. What am I saying?

Do your words sound like your co-workers, your friends on Facebook, Satan's? Or do they sound like God's? No matter what anyone else is saying, set yourself in agreement with what God says and only say what He says.

3. How easily is my perspective changed?

The goal of the enemy is always to make your problem or circumstance look bigger than God. Train yourself not to be moved off of what God says. I don't care if the lives of everyone around you are falling apart, you don't need to fear those things. Stay in faith (agreement) with what heaven says about you, about your situation and about the Kingdom of God. Cast down those thoughts that don't line up with what God says like water off a duck's back. Tell the enemy to shut up.

What you look at and think on has a huge bearing on where you'll go in life, and on whether or not you'll win in life. When Peter walked on the water with Jesus, he took his eyes off Jesus and put them on the wind and the waves (the circumstances), and he started to sink. That's what the enemy wants to do to you. Don't buy into his smokescreen. Keep your perspective in agreement with God's, and don't let the enemy change it.

Where Does Your Trust Lie?

We see so many scary things in the news, as countries' economies are failing, our government is in incredible debt and our lifestyle is threatened with impending economic doom, or so it sounds in the headlines. As more and more people depend on the government financially in some form, the entire culture and mindset of a nation changes. People trust in the government to meet their needs. Or they trust in their credit cards to get them by.

The Bible prophesies that in the last days we will see a whole lot of shaking going on, with wars and rumors of wars, famines, plagues, sicknesses and natural disasters.

As we face these sobering facts, we are not to fear. We do want to make sure our house is built on a sure foundation. Staying out of debt is a good place to start.

More importantly, we must understand the Kingdom of God and how to be led by the Spirit of God. God's Word prevails in the midst of a storm every time. I believe that He is speaking to His people now to prepare for the future (building an ark), so that we are not swept away with the rest of the world in the financial chaos that will prevail.

In the midst of financial panic, we can trust in God and His government. If we operate in faith instead of fear, He can show us how to find doors of escape, just like he led Joseph and Mary out of the path of Herod's rage, and they stayed in Egypt until it was safe to return. God will lead you by His Spirit if you will listen and trust in Him.

So, study the Kingdom of God. Learn and become confident in what Jesus paid for—a blessed life full of provision, where you're able to be generous on every occasion, you're out of debt and walking in your destiny!

> *Trust in Him and remember that this earth is not your home, anyway. Fight the good fight of faith and fulfill your assignment.*

We know that God always provides for His children! It says in His Word that it is the will of God for you to prosper and be in health even as your soul prospers. (3 John 2.)

Trust in Him and remember that this earth is not your home, anyway. Fight the good fight of faith and fulfill your assignment. But don't become so attached to this world that you forget why you are here, and it's not to live a comfortable, easy life. It's to get up and go into the battle, winning souls for God and advancing His Kingdom.

Don't get too comfortable where you are because God wants to always take you to a new place, and just like Abraham, you may not know where that is. It will take trusting Him and leaning on His Word. It will take courage.

Whose Territory Are You In?

Let me get right to the point.

You have an adversary.

He doesn't care if you're in church, or that you're going to heaven. He doesn't care if you go sing a few songs on Sunday mornings. He's already lost you. He doesn't care if there are a million people in church. He just doesn't want those "church people" to influence the world! He doesn't want you to prosper.

He just doesn't want to see you exercise your authority, discover your destiny or advance and take territory for God.

You need to have a real clear picture of Satan's intent. The world likes to be entertained by him. The culture has become desensitized to him. This isn't just some preacher's exaggeration. This is real.

As I've shared, 1 Peter 5:8 says, "Be alert and of sober mind. Your enemy the devil prowls around like a roaring lion looking for someone to devour."

Imagine you're in the bush in Africa and you hear a lion roar. You'd be afraid, right? That's a trick the enemy uses. He has no authority in your life, but he roars to make you think he does. Because he only has authority if he can make you think he does.

So he roars, and he makes circumstances appear bigger than what God says. He roars to test your agreement with heaven—to test your faith—and to see if you really have any authority.

He wants to reduce your effectiveness and stop your assignment. He wants to deceive you, to tempt you, to snare you. He wants to devour you. He wants to lure you into a place that you can't get out of. He says, "Try it one time. You're in control." You must be wise to his tactics.

The enemy is fighting to desensitize people to his existence. He convinces people that he's cuddly and warm. In my generation, we had a "friendly" ghost and a "friendly" witch. In this generation, we have people in "love" with demons and vampires. Zombies, white magic and satanic video games. The enemy is infiltrating culture to desensitize YOU.

He doesn't just come out openly and knock on your door. He sends friends who tell your kids things they shouldn't know. He whispers through a coworker about some other woman, and the things you shouldn't be putting up with from your wife. He puts those little scenes in movies for a reason. He wants to infiltrate your thoughts and make you callous against it so that it doesn't bother you.

People have a weird idea that sin is just murder and the big stuff. But the Bible says that anything outside of what heaven says is right is sin. That includes your thoughts. Sin is stepping outside of how heaven functions.

In our culture, and in the church, we've lost the fear of sin. We think we can play with it and not get burned. But when you sin, you cut yourself off. You're in enemy territory.

When I was a young believer, I was a carnal Christian. My life wasn't about the Kingdom. I went to church on Sunday, but I wasn't about God's Kingdom. I was about my own. So, God started to deal with me about some of the things I was doing. I thought, "So what? I'm not bad. I'm going to heaven. It's no big deal."

But it was a big deal. The enemy was tempting me outside of the protection of the covenant. You can't play outside of God's dominion and expect to stay in His protection. God kept dealing with me and I paid no attention. Until the day I woke up paralyzed.

Now, God didn't do that. I had willingly stepped into the enemy's territory. And I was paralyzed.

I woke Drenda up. We prayed. (Believe me, you start repenting from a lot of things when you think you're dying.) That's when God said, "Shut the door." I did, and I was healed.

It's about time the church wised up and shut the door.

Most believers think if you just whisper the name of Jesus, Satan will run off like a wounded dog. That's not how he functions. He's persistent. He waits for opportune times. He's diligent.

We have to guard our hearts and test our thoughts. We can't think about just anything. We have to pay attention. We have to cast down thoughts if they don't line up with what God says.

So be self-controlled and alert! Don't let your guard down. Let the Holy Spirit lead you and protect you and help you stay out of the enemy's traps. Shut the door.

Why Are You So Afraid?

Our perception of reality is easily warped. Like walking through a funhouse full of mirrors that distort the image, many of us have a distorted view of ourselves and of God.

Fear is the master of distortion. Let's face it: fear makes every problem seem impossibly huge. It makes us imagine things. It makes us hear scary sounds at night. It makes us lose sight of reality.

That's what happened to the disciples in Matthew 8. They had just seen Jesus heal many sick people. In fact, one of those sick people was Peter's mother-in-law, whom Jesus healed of a fever. Lepers were cured. The centurion's servant was rescued from death. Demons were cast out. You would think that the disciples' faith would be unstoppable by now. I mean, if you had seen Jesus heal so many, would you be afraid?

But just as soon as Jesus told the disciples to take Him to the other side of the lake, their faith was tested.

It says in Matthew 8:23-27:

> **Then he got into the boat and his disciples followed him. Suddenly a furious storm came up on the lake, so that the waves swept over the boat. But Jesus was sleeping. The disciples went and woke him, saying, "Lord, save us! We're going to drown!" He replied, "You of little faith, why are you so afraid?" Then he got up and rebuked the winds and the waves, and it was completely calm. The men were amazed and asked, "What kind of man is this? Even the winds and the waves obey him!"**

Jesus was sleeping. He wasn't worried about this storm. The disciples had left on this voyage at Jesus' command. In verse 18 Jesus said, "We ARE GOING to the other side." Jesus didn't say, "We are going to try to get to the other side, but we're actually going to drown on the way." But instead of standing on Jesus' word that they were going to the other side, the disciples saw the reality of the storm. They felt the waves. They heard the wind and the thunder crashes.

Many of us think that if Jesus were in the room with us, He would give us a hug and say, "I'm know you're going through a tough time, and gee, I'm so sorry. Man, you have it rough." NO! When the disciples woke Him up with their summary of the situation ("We are going to drown!") Jesus didn't say, "Group hug, guys. It was nice knowing you." He didn't feel sorry for them. He rebuked them for their lack of faith!

Instead of believing that they had authority over the storm, the disciples were amazed that the storm obeyed Jesus. Everything calmed down and they were shocked.

Hear me: what you're amazed at you'll never enjoy because it is outside of your normal thinking. Jesus wasn't amazed that the storm obeyed Him. To Him, that was normal because He knew the Kingdom of God had authority over the kingdom of the earth.

Until you exercise Kingdom authority you'll never enjoy Kingdom benefit. You'll still be bailing water out of your boat, wishing Jesus would wake up and see how bad your situation is.

> *Until you exercise Kingdom authority you'll never enjoy Kingdom benefit. You'll still be bailing water out of your boat, wishing Jesus would wake up and see how bad your situation is.*

God sees what you're going through. That's why He gave you authority over all the powers of the enemy and nothing can harm you (Luke 10:19).

Too many Christians pull out an umbrella and cope when they should be operating in Kingdom authority and releasing what God says is right. I know because I used to be an umbrella-toting, pity-party throwing, down-and-out, fearful Christian myself. Victory, joy, freedom and peace are so much more enjoyable.

Why are you putting up with that storm? Jesus is with you. Get your reality and perception from God's Word instead of this earthly realm. This earth and everything in it is subject to the King and His domain! Now, take your rightful authority over that circumstance and bring heaven's will to earth where you are.

You Are Barabbas

As human beings, we get upset at injustice. If you're like me, something in you rises up when you see something unfair happening, or you see someone hurt. Movies and television play on that. The most popular movies and shows are about good versus evil. Detective and police shows like *CSI*, and old shows like *Perry Mason* and *Murder She Wrote* are hugely popular because people love to see justice served. It's a natural instinct.

One of the things that changed my life is the realization that God operates by justice. He is the God of Justice. The definition of justice is the administration of the law or authority in maintaining the law, especially the establishment of rights according to the law. God's Kingdom is one of laws. If you get that—I mean really get that—you're life will completely change.

Religion teaches you that you can keep praying and begging and hoping something will change. But that's not the way it works. First John 5:14 says that if we ask anything according to the will of God, He hears us. If He hears us, He takes the case. We know that He is just. We can be confident that if we ask anything according to His will, He hears us. We can be confident in our legal right that justice will be served on our behalf.

See, we walk in a spiritual court of law in the earth realm. The Bible tells us that Satan is the accuser of the brethren. He says, "They belong to me!" But we have an Intercessor that paid the price for us to walk free legally.

I told you before that I used to be sick and on anti-depressants. When I received my healing, God told me not to pay attention to my emotions or feelings. It was a legal matter. It doesn't matter how you feel or what you see. What you're dealing with is a legal matter that was settled 2,000 years ago in a court of law. Don't focus on your emotions or feelings. Focus on the court records.

Your victory in this life will be determined by your understanding of justice and how to enforce it.

Psalm 89:14 tells us that justice and righteousness are the foundation of God's throne. You need to know these scriptures so that you know how to defend yourself with spiritual law. James 1:17 tells us that every good and perfect gift is from above. Romans 1:20 tells us that God doesn't change; His laws do not change.

But we can't live up to the Law. Only Jesus can. He was judged by the Law and pronounced innocent. Jesus didn't sin. He was tempted as we are, but He had a nature of light. His death was a setup. In Acts 8:32-33 we read that Jesus was deprived of justice. Jesus, the only one who wasn't guilty, was crucified as being guilty!

Satan had done something illegal in the spiritual courts of law. He deprived Jesus of justice. Jesus was innocent, but He didn't open His mouth! He was silent, willfully walking to His death. But God had a plan.

In Luke 23:18, we see how Pilate wanted to release Jesus, but the whole crowd shouted, "Away with this man! Release Barabbas to us!" (Barabbas had been thrown into prison for an insurrection in the city, and for murder.)

You are Barabbas.

Barabbas was guilty, but he was set free. He represents what Jesus did for us in His death. He paid the price in our place. Justice demanded an answer. Jesus was the answer. He was the only man on the face of the earth that could give God the legality in the earth realm. Because of His death, the Bible says that you now rule as kings and queens.

You now possess the righteousness of Jesus. You stand before God innocent, just like Barabbas walked out completely free. He could condemn himself all day long, but the legal system had declared him FREE. It's not an emotional thing. You're not saved by feelings. It has nothing to do with how you feel. This was a court case that was decided 2,000 years ago. You walk as a son or daughter of God—as if you've never sinned.

Now, Satan will try to accuse you. But 1 John 1:9 says, "If we confess our sins, he is faithful and just and will forgive us our sins and purify us from all unrighteousness." Master it. Don't let your sins take root and produce death. Confess them and release them to the Judge.

Then, wash yourself in the Word. Learn how God operates. Learn how to defend yourself. Come into agreement with justice. As you do, sin will lose its power and you'll walk free in the new life God has for you.

You Are Someone's Solution

3 John 1:2

> **Beloved, I pray that you may prosper in every way and [that your body] may keep well, even as [I know] your soul keeps well and prospers. (AMP)**

To understand how to work together with God to capture wealth and change your life, you must understand where money is and who legally controls it. It's going to come as a shock to many Christians, but...surprise! God doesn't have any money.

If you look at any piece of money, you'll find an earthly kingdom stamped on it—the nation or government that printed it—not God. So many Christians think that God is going to bring them money and they just wait for that to happen. Unfortunately, many wait a very long time with no results.

Another thing working against the believer is Satan's claim on the money in the earth realm as recorded in Luke 4:6. The only way then that God can get money to you is to help you capture it in the marketplace with concepts, ideas and strategies. WE DON'T LOOK FOR WEALTH. WE CREATE WEALTH.

As we begin to allow the Holy Spirit to lead us, we'll find that He leads us by providing us with solutions to problems that are all around us. In its most basic definition, business is simply providing answers to problems or answering the needs of people. So, look in the mirror and recognize that you are someone's solution!

By recognizing and finding solutions to life's problems, you will be postured for promotion or propelled to new places of responsibility. This repositioning will require change on our part.

To increase in position and responsibility, allow God to position you before the problems and people to whom you will bring solutions.

But this might mean that we'll find ourselves thrust into a tense situation like David was when he came to the armies and found Goliath ranting and raving. But this negative pressured situation was actually an opportunity for David, and by taking control over that problem he was forever changed and promoted. The same will be true in your case. Understand that pressure and problems are normal.

Knowing God is with you and actually training yourself to look for those opportunities that others overlook will be a key to your next victory. I remember the story that Curtis, a member of my church, told me.

Curtis had just started a new sales route for a company, and the rep that was training him was telling him about some of their clients that he serviced. Curtis asked him why their company did not have the account from the biggest company in town that would need their product. The training rep said that no one could touch that account. He said he hadn't bothered trying to get the account himself because the competitor that had it was entrenched there and had a long history.

Curtis told the trainer to drive over to that company immediately. The trainer was shocked, but drove over to the company's location. The man who was in charge of that company just happened to be there and Curtis was able to talk to him about their products. The man said that they were open to getting a bid from Curtis, and, to make a long story short, Curtis got the account—and the $40,000 a year increase in commissions that the account brought in.

To increase in position and responsibility, allow God to position you before the problems and people to whom you will bring solutions. Remember, as long as there are problems to be solved, you are assured of having as many opportunities for promotion and increased income that you want.

Today, write down a list of the problems that you encounter today. Do others have the same problem you have seen? Can you see a solution to any of them? Think on it. That solution just may be your future!

You Can't Escape People

Ever heard the saying, "Perception is reality?" Some people think it's not a true statement, but it is when it comes to leadership. And the enemy sure knows it.

It started in the Garden when he asked Eve, "Did God really say?" And, he never stopped. See, the enemy hates leadership, because he knows that God uses leaders to mold and mentor people for their destiny. If he can disrupt that, then he can alter people's lives. So, he whispers all kinds of false perceptions to corrupt your opinion of leaders so he can bring you out from under them, or people out from under you if you're a leader. Because he knows that if he can break the respect people have for a leader, he can also destroy the team.

It's been working. The world's system has perverted the image of leadership so much so that most people don't trust anyone in leadership positions, including pastors and government officials. Our culture has turned leadership into a self-serving thing, and people are fed up. There have been plenty of malfunctions in leadership in ministry, in business and in our government over the years, but just because people have failed in those offices doesn't mean that God didn't design leadership.

God raises a leader for every task He wants to accomplish. Every one of us is called to some level of leadership. As we mature in our ability to lead, God moves us on to lead bigger and better things. But you'll never get there by yourself. Wherever you go in life, whatever plans you have, will require people. God designed your destiny to include other people, so you have to be the right kind of follower and the right kind of leader or you'll never get there.

Pay attention to the perceptions you have of your leaders. Do you listen to the whispers? If someone says, "Gary doesn't like me very much. He walked down the hall and didn't say, 'hi,'" would you jump in? Would you let it alter your perception of me? You shouldn't. It's God's job to deal with the leaders, not yours. He'll even remove them if He has to. You just need to keep your heart toward where God has placed you.

> *God is going to use people in your life. You can try to avoid them, but you'll never reach the amazing destiny He has planned for you if you do.*

Your leader needs you no matter your position. In our culture, though, you're often viewed as second-class if you're not in leadership. Much like the Super Bowl, when we focus on the quarterback, how many passes he completed, the yardage he covered, etc. But the quarterback couldn't accomplish anything without his team. They're the ones blocking for him. They're doing their best with their gifts to help him with his gift. They're celebrating the fact that he can throw that pass, because they know they're all going to get a bonus check if they win. That's how we have to be in the Kingdom of God.

Remember that the next time you think your position or place is any less effective or necessary. When you stand before God, you'll have the exact same reward as the leader you're serving.

Now, if you're responsible for others, you have to be the right kind of leader. In fact, that's true even if you're only leading yourself. Be aware of people's perceptions of you. Loving God isn't enough. Plenty of people love God and still fail in life because they can't lead. You can't cause people to become indignant toward you and think you'll reach your destiny. Are you worthy of their respect? Are you worthy of their confidence? Or are you doing things like taking cash deals under the table, lying to your wife, showing up late or ignoring calls from bill collectors?

God is only as big as your word is to yourself. If you're a liar, if you don't keep your word, if you renege on your promises, you will view God as the same. Remember the story of the centurion in the Bible? He was a man of his word. If he gave an order, he knew it would be followed, so he didn't need Jesus to take any action. He only needed Jesus' Word.

If you're flaky, you won't get very far. God's not going to put you someplace where your name takes His name down. Just like if someone sees my child out there acting up, they know that's my child. What my child does or doesn't do is a direct reflection of me.

No one is perfect. We've all made mistakes. Just be humble if you do, and move toward fixing the issue. Typically, God has already been speaking to you about things you need to correct and fix because, 1.) He can't move you forward until you do, and 2.) He knows that if you don't, the enemy will use those things to destroy you.

So work at it. Lead with integrity. Live your life worthy of respect. Walk in love. Let people know you care. Be faithful to what you said you'd do. Think about the responsibility you have to those who follow you. You can't do everything you want to do. Think about it. Having 12 Lamborghinis isn't unlawful, but is it going to help me touch people's lives? Will they still be able to connect with me? We have to consider the perceptions of others and lay down some of our rights for their sakes.

God is going to use people in your life. You can try to avoid them, but you'll never reach the amazing destiny He has planned for you if you do.

You Have the Whole Estate

Several years ago, before I pastored, I drove a Peugeot that required diesel gas. Of course, there weren't many diesel gas pumps around back then. So there I was one night heading to a meeting when the gas light came on. I knew of a diesel pump in that area, but I got there and it was closed, so I just kept driving.

I started to notice how dark it was out there and how there was nothing out there—I mean nothing—and I got a little nervous. I started praying in the Spirit. I knew I probably had enough fuel to get back, but I was sure I didn't have enough to get where I was trying to go. I thought about stopping, but I didn't want to go back. I managed to push through that, but then it got even darker. I thought, "This is ridiculous. It's nothing but country out here. I have to pull over. I just have to." I pulled over with the intent of turning around and heading back. I thought I might just have enough fuel to make it back home.

Have you ever been there before? I was at a critical decision point. So, I started praying in the Spirit again, and I sensed my Spirit telling me to "keep driving, don't turn around and head towards home but keep going," but it didn't make any sense. But the urge to continue was strong, so I pulled back out on the highway and I drove maybe 100 yards and I thought, "I can't do this, this is crazy," and I pulled off the road again. I was sitting there again about to turn around and go home when I happened to glance out the passenger side window. There, tied to the fence, was a sign that said, "Diesel Fuel – 5 miles ahead" at so and so station, at some little town. I couldn't believe it! I got to that station 5 minutes before it closed. Fueled up and made my meeting.

> *God wants to train us to trust Him. He knows where everything you need is–He knows there is fuel ahead when He sends you on that trip. Trust Him!*

That's an example of how the Holy Spirit leads us. Sometimes you have to just hold on. We've all been there in the dark thinking, "I don't know. Are you sure, God? I've never been out here before." Can't you just picture the angels that night looking down on me?

"Man! He didn't stop in the right spot! Have him pull up! Come on, Gary! Look out the window! Look out the window! It's right there! Okay! Yes! He sees it!"

I really believe that's how it works in the Kingdom. God is just waiting to get something to us. God wants to train us to trust Him. He knows where everything you need is—He knows there is fuel ahead when He sends you on that trip. Trust Him!

Your Last Defeat = Your Next Victory

When was the last time you failed at something? Was it something small, or something big? Was it fun? Of course not! Failure is never fun. And it's not a cliché to say we can always learn from it. In fact, having a proper understanding of failure is vital to our success.

Honda has a proper understanding of failure. Their engineers spend 95 percent of their time studying why the lawnmower wouldn't start the first time, or why the gas mileage is higher on their new car model than it was on the old one. They know that their success lies in those failures.

We have to look at failures that same way. We're all going to make mistakes. Most of us come into God's Kingdom and we don't know how to live life, so we fail. And the enemy loves to pervert our failures. He wants us to hesitate. He tries to rehearse our failures or paint a picture of the risks. He tells us that they're permanent and we believe him. We stop. We don't move forward because we're afraid we'll fail again.

Or he blames the failure on God. That's one of his favorites. He gets us questioning God. He used it on Joshua. In Joshua 1, Moses had died and God had put Joshua in charge. So, Joshua took off. He led the people to Jericho and the walls came down. Things were working just like God had said…until we get to Chapter 7.

Everyone has a Chapter 7. That's where failure happened. There was a guy named Achan in Chapter 7. Achan had stolen some of the spoils from battle and Joshua had no clue. Unaware of Achan's failure to follow God's instructions, Joshua went ahead and sent men on to the next battle at Ai only to see his men killed.

We've all had those moments when we begin to follow Christ and something happens that doesn't match the picture, or the promise, in the Bible. If we don't understand how to deal with failure, those moments may make us lose our courage. We might hesitate, or we might set up camp and never try again, or we might just try to run back to Egypt. So, we have to understand failure and how to deal with it.

Joshua had to learn. At first, like we all do, Joshua reacted. The enemy's plan to have him blaming God worked. Joshua questioned God. Ever done that before? We all have. But God wasn't having it. He told Joshua to "GET UP!"

See, people say that they wish Jesus would just show up. Trust me, you DON'T want that. As I shared before, Jesus isn't going to show up and say, "Let's have a group hug." When the disciples freaked out that they were going to drown in the storm at sea, Jesus didn't get up and comfort them. He said, "Where is your faith?" He's going to say, "GET UP! Have you not read MY WORD? I already paid the price!" He WILL correct you.

That's exactly what God did to Joshua. He told him to get up. Then, He told Joshua exactly what had happened. See the failure wasn't just on Achan's part; it was also on Joshua's. Joshua hadn't sought instruction from God before he engaged Ai. God could have told him about Achan before they went to battle. Instead, Joshua assumed. We can NEVER assume things in the Kingdom. We can't do anything based on our past victories. The enemy is already wise to them, and he's already changed strategies.

Like Joshua, we don't have to fail. If we go to God first, failure doesn't have to happen. But, if we do fail, there are steps we can take to overcome the failure and move forward:

1. Ask God what happened. If the Word says it, it's God's will. There are a lot of variables—things like unbelief and wrong expectations—that mess with the heart and can short circuit faith. If it didn't happen, you need to ask God why.

2. Pinpoint the short circuit. Know who, what, why, when, where and how so it doesn't happen again.

3. Ask God how to fix it.

4. Get the plan on how to restore the loss.

5. Stand up and take action.

Sure, you'll be tempted to be afraid. Ignore your feelings. God commanded Joshua to be strong and courageous. You will have to be, too. You can feel afraid, but don't act like it. Remember, if you're not doing the hardest thing in your life, then you're not growing.

God has already prepared a way for you to go and succeed in a big way. Be confident to let the Holy Spirit teach you, train you and reveal unique strategies to you. Keep your vision in front of your face. Write it down! Believe it's possible; otherwise you're destined to stay right where you are.

God wants to advance His Kingdom in the earth through you. He's depending on you to overcome failure and kick butt!

Building Confidence

The dictionary defines "confidence" as the feeling or belief that one can rely on someone or something; firm trust; or the state of feeling certain about the truth of something.

What do we need to build confidence in? In God and what He has said.

First John 5:14-15 say, "This is the confidence we have in approaching God: that if we ask anything according to his will, he hears us. And if we know that he hears us—whatever we ask—we know that we have what we asked of him."

This is a very important scripture. It tells us that this is our confidence—our firm trust. If we ask anything according to the will of God, we know that He hears us. Now this phrase, *hears us*, is not referring to God hearing our voice. But instead it is referring to a legal hearing, like a courtroom. When the Bible says He hears us, it means, He takes the case. Like a judge that hears a case, whose purpose is to bring forth justice (enforcing what the law says). When God takes the case, He is going to bring forth His justice. As we read and learn what God's will is we can be confident that when we pray according to His will, that God will bring to pass His will in any situation.

As we begin to understand the confidence available to us, it will change how we live and what we expect in our lives. A key to this scripture is knowing God's will.

We have to understand the covenant in order to step into it and defend our territory, and that's no easy task. We may be confident in some situations, but when the symptoms are speaking loudly it can get really tough. It's hard to shut the door and walk away from that. One thing the enemy likes to do is to try to discourage you when you're standing on the promises of God because of what you feel. Healing is even more vulnerable to that because the feelings are screaming so loudly at you that you have to really focus on what the Kingdom of God says.

So what do we do? How do we focus? We change our picture.

We stop looking at the symptoms and we look at examples of healing—of deliverance. We change the picture we see.

We focus on the stories we know or have heard. Like the one about Doug Kirk—a marine who was in a firefight for 41 days in the largest battle in Vietnam. Doug was wounded by shrapnel, which left the nerve in his left shoulder destroyed. Doctors performed a nerve graft, but found there was still no nerve stimulation. It was dead. But Doug has full use of his arm. So what happened?

Doug believed God. There is no medical explanation. In fact, when the doctors check Doug's arm, there is still no evidence of nerve stimulation to this day.

But Doug's story of confidence gets even better. A few weeks back Doug was having some chest pains. He took some mild home remedies and started speaking to those symptoms, but they kept getting worse. So he thought he'd go over to the Urgent Care to see if they could dull the pain. They told him he was having a heart attack, but Doug knew differently. He didn't care what the symptoms appeared to be or what the EKG said—he believed God and he told them so.

The doctors called an ambulance and took Doug to the emergency room, but after 36 hours of tests they came and told him that he has the heart of a 35-year-old athlete, and they sent him home.

Doug knew something that maybe you don't. When those symptoms happened he knew to speak to them. Maybe you've never heard of that before. It's a vital part of how faith operates. Faith speaks. Doug headed it off at the pass with the words out of his mouth. He exercised spiritual authority and dominion.

Renae is another amazing example. Twenty-five years ago she was on the verge of death. Five days into her honeymoon she was in the hospital and being told to get her affairs in order. But Renae proclaimed that she was going to live. That was only the beginning of her journey. She was diagnosed with Anticardiolipin Antibody Syndrome—a disease that no one lived with for more than 2 years, and for the next 16 years Renae was constantly on the verge of death. During that time, she was rushed to the hospital 9 times and had 16 surgeries.

In 2001, when Renae weighed only 65 pounds, couldn't use her atrophied left arm or leg, and had to rely on drugs, nurses—and soon a wheelchair. She went before God. He showed her things she needed to correct, and Renae got busy renewing her mind. One day after praying and worshiping, Renae walked out her healing—literally—she ran up and down some stairs with her restored body.

There are so many pictures of healing and restoration that we can use to replace the pictures we have in our minds, and we have to do that. Ephesians tells us that we need to continually wash our minds and how we think. We live in the Kingdom of fear. We live in a dirty environment as far as faith is concerned. We have to wash our thoughts with the Word of God.

Becoming convinced takes a little bit of seasoning. You have to take the time to become convinced—to find out what God says. You have to reject thoughts that don't align themselves with the Word of God. You have to renew your mind. Fill yourself with righteous thoughts. Take the time necessary to get those scriptures into your life so that when you're in the situation you can reject it and release faith.

But what do you do when you have pain or fear yakking at you and you close your eyes and you see that picture of pain, dysfunction, lack or whatever? You go back to the Word of God. Stay there until you become convinced that it will do what it says. Get fully persuaded that God is able to do whatever He says.

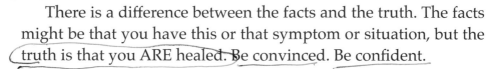

There is a difference between the facts and the truth. The facts might be that you have this or that symptom or situation, but the truth is that you ARE healed. Be convinced. Be confident.

Visit
garykeesee.com

At Faith Life Now, our mission is to share strategies for balanced living in the areas of **faith, family and finances**. We are average people who God has changed, and we have a passion to connect with real people on a practical level to encourage them toward their destiny. You can't fulfill your destiny until you get the "money thing" fixed, which is why Faith Life Now offers a wide array of practical tools and answers to life's questions. We sincerely want to see you winning in life, doing what you love to do while making an impact in this world!

Yours for the Kingdom,

Gary and Drenda Keesee

Gary & Drenda Keesee

WATCH
GARY & DRENDA KEESEE
ON

What is TeamRevolution?

Get MENTORED for Success!

When you become a valued Team Revolution Partner, you help leave a lasting impact on lives all over the world while getting mentored for change in your own life!

You will hear from Gary Keesee and a team of experts and ministers in various fields to help you change and grow in faith, family, financial success, and business.

We believe you have a special destiny and calling, and joining Team Revolution puts you in a group of people who are committed to pursuing that destiny together.

As a partner, you are vital in helping us:

- **Provide Daily TV broadcasts that reach a potential of 780 million households worldwide.**

- **Produce life-changing resources that share Kingdom strategies for successful living.**

- **Support missionaries in third world countries, feeding the poor, supporting orphanages, working to stop sex trafficking in Eastern Europe, and so much more!**

LIVES CHANGED

"Our lives and church have been revolutionized through Gary and Drenda's teaching and mentorship! Our family is continually experiencing spiritual and financial breakthrough as we incorporate the Kingdom message they teach! Our church has experienced a 30% increase in our yearly receipts, we have purchased new acreage that doubles the size of our land, and we are about to break ground on a $6 million building project! We are so grateful for the impact Gary and Drenda have made in our lives!"

- Steve and Lisa

"The Lord spoke to me and said "daughter you are blood of My blood, bring your thinking into my Kingdom." I didn't understand what it meant at the time, but after listening to your teaching you helped put the puzzle pieces together for me. You are teaching all about the Kingdom and God's way of doing things."

- Donna

"My life, marriage, family, and ministry experienced transformation when the spirit of poverty was broken, and Gary imparted a lifestyle of supernatural generosity to me."

- Leif

HOW DO I BECOME A PARTNER?

Becoming a ministry Partner is easy! Simply make your commitment via telephone, web, or mail. When we receive your first monthly contribution, you will be recognized as a Life Revolution, Destiny Team, or Inner Circle Partner, and we'll mail you your exclusive partnership package! Destiny Team and Inner Circle Partners will also receive access to your exclusive benefits available through the website.

On the Internet, go to **www.FaithLifeNow.com** and click on the "Partner" tab.

By telephone, call us at **1.888.391.LIFE**

By mail: **Faith Life Now, P.O. Box 779, New Albany, OH 43054**